M000251672

A
Transparent
Transformation

Kodeza Young

A Transparent Transformation
Published by: Kodeza Young

Edited by: Create Space
Photography by: Prentice Bethea

ISBN: 978-1-7344932-0-7
LCCN: 2017917966

Table of Contents

Introduction

What is truth? Conformity to reality or actuality? This book is my truth. There are some people near and dear to me who never knew my truth. You may think you know someone, but until you know his or her true story, you won't know who that person actually is. When you know someone's reality, then and only then can you try to begin to understand who that person is. You may be more willing to accept the way he or she acts, thinks, and speaks when you understand him or her. His or her truth makes that person who he or she is, even if you don't like it. I have been able to be very transparent with revealing my truth. It's all for a reason. I want other women to acknowledge their truths and allow their crooked paths to become straight. I want women younger and older to see my faults and my mistakes—all for what I thought was love. I don't mind if people say that I was a fool, dumb, or stupid, because I was. But if you can read my truth and decide that you want better for your life, then all of my suffering was not in vain. If I can influence one woman to expect more for herself and aim for higher, then I will be pleased.

I believe that God sat me down with pen and paper and allowed me to be transparent for the purpose of helping others. It wasn't easy. The thought of writing this book was in my head for about three years, but I never got started. Then one day, I was listening to a sermon by Juanita Bynum, and she stated that God has given each of us something to not just benefit ourselves, but others as well. It's as though she was speaking directly to me. She said, "What has God given you to do that you have not started on?" That's when I decided to start writing. I wrote during my spare time and finally completed the book a year later. You would think that I would have gotten started typing right away, but that didn't happen. I was heartbroken when a friend of mine passed. She was a special lady, and she was going to help me type the book and get it ready for publication. She was very smart, and I was counting on her, so when she left this world, I felt alone with my book. So after about a year, I got started typing. Well, I don't type very fast, and it was difficult to get help, so I did the best I could. You're now reading the finished product.

The Bible says that the truth shall make you free (John 8:32), and as I wrote my truth, I became free. I hadn't realized that after so many years, I was still harboring resentment in my heart. This book helped me to forgive and release those who I believed caused me pain. I know that I will be judged and criticized by some, but that's OK. I know that some people will not want to accept my truth or the role that they played in my truth, and that's OK also. I just thank God for never leaving me and allowing my truth to be revealed.

Chapter One
The Foundation

In my early years, I spent most of my time with my maternal grandparents, Catherine and Roy Gunter. My parents, Ethel and Sidney Young Jr., were married at young ages. These young, new parents were trying to find their way in life. Both were either working or in school. I grew up calling them by their first names, and people would often ask me why as I got older. My only response was, "I guess that's what they taught me, because kids aren't born calling their parents by their names." Well, after being married for seven or eight years, my parents decided to divorce, which afforded me even more time to spend with my grandparents.

My grandparents were and are the best grandparents ever. I am the firstborn grandchild, and my loving grandfather calls me "number one." My grandparents made sure I was on the church bus every Sunday morning for Sunday school. They made sure I was in the sunshine choir at church. Gospel Light United Holiness Church, where my godparents were the bishop and first lady, was our family church. My grandparents have been longtime active members of this church. My grandfather has been a deacon of this church for many years, and my grandmother is now one of the mothers of the church. We were in church every Sunday. Often, after morning worship service, we would go across the street to the church annex for some good home-cooked soul food and then go back to church for the evening service. We went to Bible study and church meetings, and my God, if it was a revival you knew that you would be in church, tarrying all night and every night of the revival. The foundation was being laid (Prov. 22:6).

I had a good life in my grandparents' home. For five years I was the baby in the house. I had an aunt (Joyce) and an uncle (Leroy "Lil' Daddy"), who both also helped to care for me. After the first five years of my life, my grandparents decided to do it all over again. Yes, Granny got pregnant. They already had three children (the youngest was eighteen years old), and I was grandbaby number one. Well, my little aunt Madina was born, and oddly enough, I wasn't jealous. I was the perfect little helper. I was only five, but I remember climbing up in the rocking chair with the new baby, putting the covers over our heads, and rocking her to sleep. She was so adorable. We were able to grow together for about four or five years.

Although my parents were divorced, they still managed to get pregnant with my brother Damon. Before Damon was born, my parents decided to move to Georgia and give it another try. Whatever happened in Georgia was a mystery to me because I wasn't there, but by the time I moved, my dad wasn't living there anymore. And that was truly the end of them trying to be together. Well, as far as I know.

So now I was in Georgia, the big A. We really lived in College Park, but everybody calls it Atlanta. Once again, I found myself being the perfect little helper with my brother. He was the most gorgeous baby you could ever imagine. Everyone wants a fat, juicy baby, and that's what he was. His yellow skin was smooth, and his eyes were dreamy. You just couldn't help but fall in love with him. I would feed him, change his diapers, play with him, and put him to sleep. I carried him around so much before he could walk that people would say I had a permanent indention in my hip from his resting there.

My mother was a hard worker. I always remember her having two jobs, and somehow—in between her jobs—she managed to get married two other times. Her second husband was a police officer for the city of College Park. He was pretty cool to me as a young child, but I guess I didn't know everything about him that my mother knew. Although my mother's skin complexion was very light, she was not white, and he had a love for white women. I remember being with my mother on one adventure to catch him in the act of cheating. On this particular occasion, we found him in some apartments with some white woman. My mother had this woman shaking in her boots. I don't remember all that was said, but it resulted in my mother grabbing her and getting in a few good licks before anyone could get her off. There was another incident in which she came upon him in a hotel room, and she ended up shooting her gun. She didn't hit anything or anyone. Needless to say, this marriage was very short-lived. I often wonder if my mother's actions were the start of a generational curse.

Now here comes husband number three. Will this be the one? Once again, my mother was drawn to a police officer. It was something about those uniforms. Tee Cassells was employed by the Clayton County Sheriff's department. He is an ex-marine and a chaplain to the soldiers. Many people may not know this, but, yes, he was a minister to the soldiers. Although my biological father (husband number one) was still an active and present force in my life, he was in another state (North Carolina). Tee came along and became my second father. I felt really blessed; some people don't even have one father present, but I now had two.

During my early teen life, I was a somewhat normal child. I didn't get into much trouble probably because I never got caught doing wrong. I was still helping to take care of my brother. My mom and Tee were working so much, it became my responsibility to make sure my brother got home from school, did his homework, and ate dinner. I always believed that we had a good life. We never wanted for anything. The refrigerator was always full. My mother shopped for shoes and clothes all the time, so our closets were always full. But in the midst of it all—school for my brother and I, work for my mother and Tee, living in a nice condominium, and having everything we thought we needed—there was one very important missing factor. God. The spiritual and inspirational direction and guidance were no longer there. My mother grew up in Gospel Light United Holiness Church, just as I had, and she believed in God and was a Christian. But we never went to church here in Georgia for many years. Maybe she was churched out, or maybe she was tired from working so much, or maybe it was because Granny wasn't around to guide and direct us. But for whatever reason, we didn't go to church, and I think that missing factor had a major impact on our family dynamics.

Chapter Two
The First Love

Age fourteen was a monumental age for me. I lost my virginity to my nineteen-year-old boyfriend. Most people might think that was just downright wrong. Don't judge me, because truth be told, everyone reading this has not been an angel all of his or her life. I know this to be true, because the Bible says we were born into sin (Ps. 51:5). Anyway, at age fourteen, I experienced the first true love of my life, Rodney. Rodney was tall, dark, and fine, like a big piece of chocolate! I would not have wanted to experience this with anyone else. He was older, but he genuinely cared for me. Rodney was so gentle and loving with me even though he was a roughneck. Yes, a roughneck. He knew the streets, and he taught me a lot. Rodney schooled me on relationships and men. I remember him telling me, "If a dude don't care nothing about you, he will whisper anything in your ear just to get in your pants, Lil' Dirty." That's what he used to call me: "Lil' Dirty." Rodney schooled me on lies that men would throw at you. He was truly instrumental in my life. The first time we made love was incredible. Rodney made sure that I felt special and comfortable. No, I wasn't his first, but he was mine, and he took on the role of my first and played it very well. My mother was at work one day, and we took advantage of the opportunity of being alone. Rodney gently laid me down on the sofa and proceeded to caress my body. Every touch of his lips made my body melt. Then that moment came when he entered into my body, and all I could think was how much I loved him. Yes, I loved him. My first love was so sweet and so innocent. Our romance lasted for several months, and the lovemaking got better and better. Rodney and I made many memories together.

We began to get too comfortable with being at home alone. Rodney was in my bedroom one day when my mother decided to come home from work early. That was a crazy day. I called my mother's friend to get her to talk on the phone with my mother while I tried to sneak Rodney out of the house. While my mother was on the phone, Rodney climbed out of my window, jumped past the dog, and ran down to the street. We were both pretty scared of getting caught that day because Ethel Mae did not play, and you did not want to get caught up in her wrath.

Rodney and I shared some good memories other than sex. Rodney also was the first person I smoked weed with. Now you may think that sounds crazy, but looking back on those times, I am glad I wasn't experimenting with someone who would have gotten me high and did whatever they wanted with me and then left me in the woods for dead. I am glad that I had a Rodney in my life.

When my mother found out about Rodney and about the fact that he was older and had a car, she informed me that I was not allowed to ride in his car. Really, Mother? I have a boyfriend with a car, and I can't get a ride to school? Well, on many occasions Rodney would meet me along the way and give me a ride to school anyway. I remember being in a beauty pageant at school, and guess who showed up to show me some love? Yes, Rodney— he was right there, cheering me on. My mother wasn't very receptive to him in the beginning, but he was very charming, and she eventually came to like him.

I experienced my first heartbreak with this young man. No, he didn't cheat on me, he never said a harsh word to me, and he never made me feel bad about anything. I never got pregnant by him, and he never transmitted any sexual diseases to my body. But he made one very serious mistake. This mistake not only affected his life but mine as well.

One night we were talking on the phone, and he was about to take one of his friends home. I had this bad feeling, and I asked him not to go several times, but he assured me that it wouldn't take long and that he would call me back as soon as he returned home. I still remember that phone call like it was yesterday. I begged him to stay on the phone and talk to me until I fell asleep like we had done so many times before, but he didn't. I waited and waited, but that phone call never came. I felt that something wasn't right, but I didn't know exactly what.

I got up the next morning and headed to school like I did every other morning. By the time I got to school, gossip was buzzing all around. Rodney had never attended our school, but everyone knew him because his younger brother was a student there. I remember someone asking me if I had heard what happened to Rodney. That's when I got the awful news that he was in jail. He had been arrested the night before, which is why the phone call never came. I was devastated. I couldn't talk to him. I didn't know when he would be released, and I was going crazy. After a few days, I decided to tell my mother about the situation. I could tell that she was disappointed. I failed to mention that this was not his first time being in trouble with the justice system. My mother knew of his past, and that's why she was skeptical of him in the beginning, but everyone deserves a second chance. I knew she cared because she sent someone to check on him in the jail. That person came back and reported to us that he was able to speak with him, and Rodney was honest about his actions. He sent his apologies not only to me but also to my mother. He had already been on probation, and with this arrest, his probation was revoked, and he had four years to serve in prison.

This began a downward fall with the rest of the men I would encounter in my life. I always felt in my heart that if he had not been taken away from me, my life would not have been filled with so much pain. He was the only man I was involved with who never intentionally caused me pain while we were together. Maybe it was because we were so young or because we weren't together very long that Rodney never hurt me—or maybe it was because he really cared about me. The answers to all these "maybes" would remain unknown, because Rodney had to go away. Rodney decided that he didn't want me to put my life on hold while he was gone, and he basically told me in a letter that he could not be in touch with me since he would not be able to see me for a long period of time. I cried for quite some time because I had lost my first love, my first everything, and I didn't even get a chance to see him again to say goodbye. I thought that I was going to cry my eyes out, and all I could think about was that if he had listened to me that night, none of this would be happening. But it was too late, and so that was that. We didn't see or speak to each other for another three or four years.

I got my very first job right before I turned fifteen. A friend of my mother's hired me as a waitress at Po Folks on Old National Highway, College Park. For so many years I was sheltered by people in Clayton County. The only schools I had attended were in Clayton County, and that was pretty much all that I knew. Now I was exposed to different individuals. The people I worked with went to M. D. Collins, Therrel High School, Harper High School, and others. This was a new and exciting journey for me. I learned how to ride the MARTA transit from Godby Road to Old National. We lived in Yorktowne condominiums, so it was a pretty good walk to the bus stop on Godby. No matter how long the walk was, I enjoyed catching the bus and having a job.

Po Folks is where I met my road dog, Ashanti, who was also one of the best cheerleaders M. D. Collins had ever seen. She had beautiful, dark, flawless skin, and she was in perfect shape from cheering. We just instantly became friends. The two of us together could have potentially gotten into a lot of trouble if we had gotten caught. We used to sneak out of the house and take her mom's car to go meet our boyfriends or go to parties, clubs, or whatever else we wanted to do. One time, I thought she was totally crazy! We had to sneak past her stepfather, who was sleeping on the couch, to get through a back door or window. My heart was pounding so hard I thought the sound of my heart alone would wake him up. But we made it not only that night but many more. We would always get back at sunrise, and no one ever knew we were gone. Ashanti would always drive with a Bible in her lap. One time I asked her about the Bible, and she said it was for protection. I asked, "From what?"

She said, "Because I am driving without a license."

Although we were fifteen years old, I never thought about her having a driver's license or learner's permit. So we were sneaking out of the house and driving and riding around illegally. God was protecting us from hurt, harm, and danger.

I remember one of the many concerts we attended was New Edition. We decided to skip school the day of the concert to find them. We met at one of the MARTA train stations and started our adventure. The concert was at the Omni (in downtown Atlanta), so we figured New Edition would be staying at the Omni Hotel. We managed to get through a service entrance, and we gave a sob story to an elderly man who worked there. We told him that we were friends of New Edition from their hometown, and we wanted to surprise our friends with a visit. He believed us, and we were taken through the kitchen and up the service elevators to the floor where they were staying. The gentleman left us after he told us what rooms they were in. He didn't want to be seen with us and possibly get into trouble. We knocked on the first door, and no one responded. We knocked on the second door, and Michael Bivins opened the door with a shower cap on his head, a towel wrapped around his waist, and a toothbrush in his mouth. When he saw us he started smiling, but before we could say anything, his bodyguard came up behind us from out of nowhere and said "Can I help you ladies?" and that was the end of that. We enjoyed the concert that night with our own little secret that we had seen at least one of the members of New Edition earlier that day. I can say that Ashanti kept me pretty busy and kept excitement in my life.

Chapter Three
The Beginning of the Love of My Life

I met the love of my life when I was fifteen years old. He may not want his name revealed, so for the purpose of this book, he will be referred to as the love of my life. We didn't start dating until I was sixteen years old. I only had the pleasure of being in high school with him for six months, because he graduated before I did. I was relatively quiet in high school. After the love of my life graduated early, we really started spending time together, which was odd, because when we were in school together, our time had been limited. This was probably because he had too many girls and couldn't mingle with all of us at the same time. We started dating officially—he was my guy, and I was his girl. Teenage sweethearts. I thought it would last forever. We were young, dumb, and careless, and I got pregnant. I was so scared, and I did not want to face my mother. Surprisingly, she did not kill me, but she told me that the love of my life and I had some decisions to make. Well, we considered the facts. I was still in high school and working at Mrs. Winners. He had graduated from high school and was working at Pizza Hut. We did not feel that we made a good combination at that time to be parents of anyone. So we chose the option of abortion. The love of my life was very supportive. He went with my mother and me to the clinic and back home. He never left my side. After we had returned home, he went to the pharmacy to get my prescriptions and brought me back flowers to help me feel better. That would be the first and last time that I would receive flowers from the love of my life.

Over the next year, we became thick as thieves. We were always together, and I fell in love. When he escorted me to my junior prom, I was the happiest girl in the world. A year later, the love of my life decided to become a military man. He joined the navy. I couldn't believe it; my man was leaving me. We had become what I thought was best friends. We talked and saw each other every day. I truly loved that man. When he left for boot camp in California, I cried for a month. We wrote to each other constantly during his time at boot camp. When it was time for his graduation from boot camp, he wanted me to travel with his mother to California to see him graduate. He was graduating the same weekend as my senior prom. Wow! What's more important: my senior prom, or going to see the love of my life graduate from boot camp? You know which one I chose. I figured that the love of my life and I had gone to my junior prom together, so missing the senior prom to see him graduate from boot camp was OK. He became the priority in my life. I was so proud of him, and he paid for my plane ticket. I was surprised that my mother allowed me to go. His mom and I boarded a plane, and we were on our way to San Diego, California, to see him graduate.

When I first saw him, words can't describe what I felt. It had been three months since I had been with the love of my life. We enjoyed the time that we were able to spend together. Three months without your man is a long time, so you know we had to make up for lost time! The visit came to an end, and his mother and I headed back home while he headed to school for his job classification.

I got a phone call one day that Rodney had been released from prison and was back home. I had mixed emotions. All of a sudden I thought about how we had been before he left. We had not seen each other in three or four years. People change in that amount of time. I don't remember how we got in touch with each other, but we arranged a time to meet. I was very nervous, excited, and overwhelmed with confusion. I went to see him at his mother's house, and the moment I laid eyes on him was indescribable. The years that he had been gone had done him some justice, because he was finer than he was when he had left. (How can that be possible?)

When we hugged, I could have just melted in his arms. Then we kissed, and nothing else mattered at that moment. It felt just as loving as it did the first time we had been together. I wanted Rodney to throw me down on the floor and give me the opportunity to show him that I was a big girl now. But he didn't, and it stopped at the kiss. At that moment, I decided that the love of my life was more important to me than Rodney. I turned down the only man who had never intentionally caused me any pain. I should have taken control of the moment and thrown him down on the floor and made up for lost time, but I maintained my composure. He knew about the love of my life, because he had been keeping up with me through the grapevine. So we talked, and I told him that I was serious about the love of my life. I can't remember how our meeting ended, but I know that was one of the hardest days of my life. Many times I regretted the outcome of that meeting. You will see why later.

My high school graduation was quickly approaching, and I found out that the love of my life would not be able to come home and share in this occasion. For my graduation, my family traveled from North Carolina (Dad and Mom) and Virginia (my grandparents and Auntie Madina). As I was sitting on the field, looking up into the stands, not only did I see my family, but I also saw my first love. Yes, Rodney was there. Now I can't say for sure that he was there to see me, but I still got a warm feeling in my heart knowing that he was there. That night some friends and I got a hotel room on Old National and partied the night away. Everybody had rooms that night. We were not the only school graduating, so other schools were joining in on the festivities, too.

A few weeks after graduation, the love of my life headed home, but he would not tell me he was coming. I was working the drive-through at Mrs. Winners when I turned around and saw this tall, dark, fine dude with blue shorts and a cut-off shirt that said "Navy." He had on dark shades, and I couldn't really tell that it was the love of my life. He had not had this banging body the last time I had seen him. He had been a little skinny runt the last time we were together. When I recognized who he was, I walked over to him to hug him, but he wasn't interested in a hug. He wanted to go outside and talk. He proceeded to tell me about some he-said-she-said bull crap about me and some little short boy, and he believed it, so he had to let me go. At that moment I should have walked off, called it a loss, and found Rodney. I was devastated. He left me standing there while he jumped in his car and drove away. I started shaking all over. I went back inside and told my supervisor that I had to go home. There was no way that I could continue to work; I could not stop shaking. I should have run as far away from him as I could. But remember, he was the love of my life and what I thought was my best friend. I don't know how we ended up talking, but we did, and that started many years of us playing this back-and-forth game.

The love of my life stayed in the navy for four years. He was stationed in Charleston, South Carolina, which wasn't that far away. We saw each other quite often. I was enrolled in college and working. When he wasn't home, my friends and I were hanging out and hitting the clubs. I started going to the clubs when I graduated high school. No, I wasn't old enough to be in the club, but they didn't ask for identification. Once you get in the club, of course you are going to drink; at least, that's what I did.

My mother and Tee bought me my first car one Christmas. It was a black Mercury Capri. Since I was partying quite regularly, I felt compelled to go to church. I would pick up one of my friends in Decatur, Georgia, and we would go to her church. Remember, "train up a child the way they should go and when they grow older they shall not depart" (Prov. 22:6). I grew up in a Holiness church, so as a child I always heard hooping preaches. I saw people falling out in the spirit and shouting all over the church. The church that my friend and I attended was a Baptist church. The pastor changed my mind concerning the word of God. He was intelligent, spoke with clarity, and could break down a scripture and bring it up to have present-day relevance. I learned to listen carefully so that I could gain understanding of what the Bible was saying. I was not saved, but I knew that in the midst of all the sinful acts that I was committing, I needed to be in church to ask God for forgiveness. I partied, but I made sure that I was in church on Sunday morning. I was going out with my friends and having fun, but something was missing: the love of my life. I wanted to get married and move with him so that I could be a military wife. That was out of the question; he always had some excuse not to get married, based upon other people's experiences. He would tell me stories of how navy wives would cheat on their husbands when they were deployed out to sea. He would mention the awful Dear John letters that others had received while they were away from home.

The love of my life was about to leave for the first of two six-month deployments on the friendly seas, so I figured that if I could be good for the six months and prove to him that I would not send him a Dear John letter, maybe he would marry me. I was on a mission to prove my love and to prove that I would not hurt him. I wrote him almost every day, sometimes twice a day. I stayed faithful, and there was no way you could get me to look at another man. I was really trying hard.

The first sixth-month tour ended, and I went with his family to welcome him home. We met the ship as it docked in Charleston, South Carolina. Even though there were not any problems while he was gone, he still refused to marry me. I should have seen the signs then. Shortly after he returned, I discovered why he did not want to be anyone's husband. I found pictures and phone numbers of several different women. But of course there was always a good excuse. He seemed to have his women pretty tamed, because they would never drop a dime on him. Yes, I was that one; I called numbers looking for information, and they were always close-lipped. So I allowed myself to be stupid and believe that they were just friends. Everything that Rodney taught me about men just seemed to go right out of the window when it came to the love of my life. I was stupid for this man. I gave up on being a navy wife, but he was still the love of my life. When he was not in Georgia, he was with whoever, but when he was home, he was with me.

By the time he went on his last six-month tour, I was tired of the other-women business, so he did get a "Dear John" letter. At that point, I figured, why should I care? He wouldn't make me his wifey, he was cheating, and he wasn't here. I needed a break from all of his stress.

My mother had a friend whose brother-in-law had just moved to Georgia from New Orleans. He was involved in some illegal activities that resulted in the death of his best friend, and now he needed a new beginning. We were introduced over the phone, and we had a few conversations before deciding to meet up one night at a club. It was my twenty-first birthday celebration, and I was not really sure if I wanted some man around me whom I didn't know. But when I laid eyes on him, all I could think was, *Gorgeous! Sexy!* I forgot about the love of my life. It was now all about Mr. New Orleans. My mother's friend assured her that he had a way with the ladies and that I would never think about the love of my life again. My mother knew me quite well, and she told her friend that no matter what happened, the love of my life would always be around. They went back and forth about the situation, and I found it to be quite funny.

Mr. New Orleans and I spent a lot of time together. He was staying with his sister and brother-in-law at the time, and I loved to visit during dinner. Every weekend, he would say, "Are you coming over?" and I would reply, "Is your sister cooking?"

He would say, "Koosie, come on now, it don't matter if she cooking. You coming to see me!" He always let me know how beautiful he thought I was and how much he wanted to be with me. Sometimes I thought that he was just overwhelmed from being in a new environment and lonely inside because of the loss of his best friend. I was the first woman he was introduced to after moving to Georgia, so I thought maybe I wasn't all that great and that he was just in a vulnerable state. He is the only one who knows for sure what his feelings were at the time. After a few months of dating, we decided to take a trip to New Orleans. This would be his first time returning home since the day of his best friend's funeral. I could tell that it was an emotional time for him, so I was trying to be supportive. Two of my friends traveled with us to receive the Sin City experience. We all stayed at his mom's house and experienced some good New Orleans hospitality. This was my first time in New Orleans, and I enjoyed every moment (good food, good partying). His mother cooked for us every day. We had fish, gumbo, stuffed peppers, barbeque, dirty rice, and the list goes on and on. I did not have a lot of details about his illegal activities, but I noticed that when we walked Bourbon Street, his friends were all around. As we walked, there were two guys in front of us, one on each side and two in the back. When we were in the club, they were never more than four or five feet away, and one of them was always posted at the entrance of the club. I started thinking that my life could really be in danger. Bullets don't have names on them. Well, I drank so much alcohol that the thought of danger escaped my mind eventually. I think I stayed drunk most of the trip to mask my fears. He also drank pretty heavily. One night at the club, he drank so much that he started bumping and grinding on me and whispered in my ear that he wanted to make love to me on the dance floor. I had on a short skirt, and he said that it would be easy access, and no one would know. OK, he was joking, but he did give me something to think about for the rest of the night until we got back to his mother house. Let's just say we had a good night.

While we were there visiting, his family did not hesitate to inform me of how much he talked about me. His sisters said that they had never seen him act so concerned for a woman before. The pressure was on, because he really wanted to be my man, but in the back of my mind, I was not over the love of my life. Mr. New Orleans always reminded me how much he enjoyed being with me and how beautiful he thought I was. He even brought me flowers. I hoped that he could make me forget about the love of my life.

The six months were coming to an end, and the love of my life would be heading home soon. I received a phone call from the love of my life's mother. She informed me that he would be coming home, and she wanted me to travel with her and her family to greet her son as his ship docked. I told her that we had not spoken in a while and that he did not want to see me. I was the one who had sent the Dear John letter, so why would he want to see my face when he returned? She didn't care about all of that nonsense: "My son wants to see you, and no other woman is going with me to see him, so be ready when it's time to go."

So if I decided to take that trip, how was I going to explain that to Mr. New Orleans? I felt bad because I was convinced that he really did care about me. But, once again, you know who I chose: the love of my life. That was a big mistake, but we have to live with the choices we make. I had to tell Mr. New Orleans that the love of my life was coming home, and I had decided to go and see him when his ship pulled into dock. This meant that our love affair was over. Mr. New Orleans was very upset about my decision. He reminded me that the love of my life was the man who had cheated on me and treated me wrong. He wanted to know why I wanted someone who did not treat me better. That is a question that I was not able to give a logical answer. I was young and believed that love could conquer all. Mr. New Orleans and I did not speak for many years after this conversation.

There I was, traveling with the love of my life's family to welcome him back to the United States. We arrived in Charlestown, South Carolina. I didn't know what to expect. Did he know that I was coming? He had been writing to other women while he had been away, so any of them could have been in Charlestown to greet him. What was I getting myself into? When we finally boarded the ship and saw him, he was hugging and speaking with everyone except me. I just stood there looking at him, thinking, *Boy, stop trying to act hard, and kiss me!* He made me wait for a while before he would even make eye contact with me. Finally, he walked over and asked what I was doing there. My response was "I came to see you." I felt that he knew he loved and had missed me while he was trying to make me suffer.

That night, we discovered our love all over again. It was as if I had never written that Dear John letter. I suppose that I forgot about his cheating, and he forgot that I had dumped him at sea. After we reunited, either his cheating slowed down, or he just got better at hiding what he was doing. He probably just got better at hiding his wrongdoings. But one thing that did not slow down was his drinking. He became a heavy drinker and an insomniac. I think that he was fighting some serious demons. My relationship with him continued to be a work in progress, as did my relationship with his family. His mom seemed as though she loved me as her own daughter. I would eat at her house several times a week, and when the love of my life was home, she would even allow me to spend the night at her house so that I could be with my man. If there was a wedding, funeral, party, or any family event, his mother would call me to accompany her and the family.

Although the love of my life and I were back together, I would still party with my friends when he was not home. I came across a money-making opportunity in the clubs. No, I was not a stripper. I was slim with a small waist, and I had some big, thick legs. I found that I could make some money wearing a miniskirt and a pair of stilettos. I started dancing in miniskirt contests. The first contest that I entered, I was the third-place winner. The reward was a tall trophy and a few dollars, but I wanted that first-place $500. The club was called Deon Sanders, and it was located on Windy Hill Road.

I was determined to get that money. I waited for a few weeks and returned to the club, where I claimed my $500. That was the start of a dependency that I did not need. Whenever I wanted or needed extra money, I would find out what club was hosting the next miniskirt contest. When I hit the clubs, I was drinking a lot in order to feel comfortable about being in that environment. That was a good indication the clubs was not where I was supposed to be. I was able to really dance after drinking forty ounces of beer before arriving to the club, and I would still have more drinks after I arrived. By the time I finished drinking and dancing, there was absolutely no way that I should have been able to drive and make it home safely. There were nights that I had no idea how I made it home. I would wake up the next morning in my bed, clueless as to how I got there. I later realized that angels had been driving my car, because as intoxicated as I was, I never hit anyone or anything. I was never stopped by the police, and my mom never knew my condition when I got home. There is an old saying that God takes care of babies and fools. I fell in the fool category. Pray that God never takes his hands off your life. When I think back on so many occasions, I knew that it had to be God protecting me. God had a plan for my life that I could not see and had never even thought about. Thank you, God!

My last venture with miniskirt dancing came when I needed money for school. I was a college student, and classes were starting, but I did not have the money for my books. I called one of my friends and told her that I needed to get to a miniskirt contest. We met and went to Club Hollywood. As I was dancing on the stage, a young man dangled a hundred-dollar bill from his hand and gestured for me to come over and dance for that money. He laid the money on the floor in front of him and waited for me to come and get it. Yes, I danced my way over to him so that I could retrieve that hundred-dollar bill. As I picked the money up from the floor, a very strong feeling came all over my body. I was in the club, drunk, dancing my but off, and I had thought that I was having a good time until I suddenly felt degraded and disrespected. At that moment, my self-esteem dropped to the floor, and for the first time in my life, I felt worthless. I am not judging people for what they do, but for myself, I realized that this type of activity was not for me. I remember thinking to myself that this was not how I was raised. I come from a good family. My grandmother and mother taught me to be better than this. I was ashamed and embarrassed, and I felt dirty. That night was the last time that I entered a miniskirt contest. I stopped just in time, because these contests started getting really out of control. The women started stripping right down to their bare butt cheeks. That was not for me, so I was glad that I had retired.

When I first started taking college courses, my major was in nursing. The math and science courses were too difficult in my opinion, and that was probably because I was partying and hanging in the clubs far too often. I decided to change my major to psychology, and that worked out better for me, because my grades in psychology courses were As and Bs. The reading was much easier to follow, and the subjects just seemed more interesting than algebra and anatomy.

The time came for my graduation from college. Once again, I found out that the love of my life would miss another graduation. This was beginning to be a pattern. Later you will see how many important occasions he will be absent from, and not all are because of military life. All of my parents and stepparents were at my graduation, and they helped me to celebrate this accomplishment in my life with a nice dinner at Houston's. Although I had a degree in psychology, I never found a job in that field. Someone should have informed me that you really need a master's degree in this field to get a decent job.

Chapter Four
The Grown Life

Four years passed, and a lot of things happened. The love of my life and I both grew up and somewhat apart, but we were not able to recognize it at that time, or maybe I just couldn't or didn't want to recognize it. Before he left to join the navy, he was my best friend, and I was hoping that he still held that title. You may think that I was crazy because I still wanted to be with him after all of the cheating, but we were both young. When you are young, you are allowed to make mistakes, explore, and be adventurous. You only live once, right? But by the time you reach your midtwenties, things should start to change. That's the time to consider career choices, family, and the future. That's the time to start settling down. The love of my life completed his four years in the navy and was now home. After being home and finding a job, he moved into his first apartment. We had another brief breakup, and when we got back together, I think the offer for me to live with him came out of guilt. Guilt or not, I didn't care; I jumped at the opportunity to live with him. My mother knew of our living arrangements, but I would never tell my father or grandparents that I was living out of wedlock with a man.

We were living together, working, playing, and having fun. During this time, I met one of the best friends that I would ever have in life. Ms. Kenya was dating the love of my life's best friend. When we first met, I remember saying to myself, "Look at this yellow, long-haired heifer. She think she's cute." Actually, she *was* cute, and her long hair was real, not a weave. Later, we laughed about our first encounter, because she had some thoughts about me also. We became the best of friends in just a short time.

We all were attending the same church, where her boyfriend's uncle was the pastor. (Remember the pastor, because he becomes a very important part of this book.) The church was just getting started, and we had services on Sundays at 2:00 p.m. I decided to stop going to Decatur for church, and I joined this church that we all were attending. I was young, but when I attended church services, I listened to every little detail, and I learned to give God 10 percent of my earnings (tithes).

We would party on Saturday nights and sleep late on Sundays without worrying about being late for church. I remember one Saturday night we were leaving Kenya and her boyfriend's apartment, headed to the club. We both walked across the living room floor in our miniskirts and high heels; we were fierce. From the corner of the room, this deep voice said, "I will see you ladies in church tomorrow, right?" We almost jumped out of our heels. It was one of the elders of the church, the pastor's brother. That was a disadvantage of being best friends with someone who was about to marry your pastor's nephew. Every time I visited her, I saw somebody from church.

When I was twenty-two years old, I decided to stop taking birth control pills. After taking these pills for four years, I thought that I would still be covered from pregnancy for at least a few months. Well, I was wrong. I stopped taking the pills in November 1992, and I got pregnant December 31, 1992. Yes, I know exactly when I got pregnant. The love of my life and I celebrated New Year's Eve with a couple of bottles of champagne, and we went all in. We were getting drunk and making a baby. Happy New Year! I never would have imagined getting pregnant that quickly, but it happened. Almost three months after our New Year's celebration, I became sick. I went to the emergency room because I felt so bad. My immune system was low, and it was affecting my health. I was vomiting after eating certain foods, but I just attributed it to having a cold. While in the emergency room, there were several test that were a part of my evaluation. The doctor came into my room and said "I was waiting on your last test results, and now I have them all. Everything looks good, except you have a urinary tract infection, which we will treat with some IV antibiotics. Now, for your last test result,"—he paused—"you're pregnant."

My response was "*No, I am not!*" The doctor started laughing at my response and reassured me that I was definitely pregnant. Wow, for the second time, we were pregnant. I was going to be a mommy, and the love of my life was going to be a daddy. Our mothers were going to be first-time grandmas, which equals lots of help.

My first ob-gyn visit revealed that I was already about three months pregnant. At about five months into my pregnancy, my morning sickness was really bad. It was supposed to have been over by that point, but it wasn't. I knew that I would get sick every morning after I ate, so I would wake up at six in the morning to cook breakfast, eat, and then get sick before going to work. That was the start of my day. During this time, I was a teller at a local bank, and I worked the typical nine-to-five hours. The love of my life had to be at work earlier than me, so he did not get to witness all of the morning vomiting. He didn't seem to be very supportive, and it became very apparent whenever his navy friends would come into town to visit. We lived in a one-bedroom apartment with one bathroom, and at least three or four of his friends would visit at a time. Well, guess what I was forced to do? Get out of the apartment while they were visiting. Yes, I had to go back home and think of a good lie to tell my mom so that I wouldn't look like a complete idiot about being put out for the weekend for his friends. This was so disrespectful to me, but whenever I mentioned it, I was reminded that I did not pay rent there, and he had the last say. I always thought to myself that a one-bedroom apartment was not enough space for four or five grown men. They could have gotten a hotel room, and he could have met them some place without putting me out of my home. They were all still in the navy, so surely between four or five guys, they could have split the bill on a hotel room. Well, tension began to build up every time they visited, and anger inside of me got even stronger with every visit. I was young, pregnant, hormonal, and evil. While they were out on the town, enjoying Atlanta, I would return to the apartment and do all sorts of things that they did not know about. Let's just say their personal belongings were not safe around me. Finally, I had had enough, so I called one of my friends to help me pack up all of my belongings to move back to my parent's home. I was seven months pregnant, going up and down stairs to load my car, and he and a friend just stood there watching my friend and me load my car without offering a single hand of help. We finished loading my car with my things and drove away.

Back home with my mom, Tee, and my little brother. Seven months pregnant and no baby daddy. My mom was glad to have me back home, because she wanted to be able to be close to the baby. About a month of being back home, the love of my life and I started communicating again after I was over being furious. We were not officially back together, but if you are pregnant, you are not really fair game on the market, if you know what I mean, so I started to spend time with him again.

I would often tease everyone about going into labor, and they would believe me until I said "Just kidding!" But the time came when I realized that I should have not been crying wolf.

I worked up until the day my baby was born. That Saturday I went to work, and when I completed my shift, I went to my pastor's wedding. After the wedding, I stopped by to see the love of my life, and we had a hot sexual evening. I headed home, and he probably headed to the club. Around four o'clock in the morning, I woke up feeling uncomfortable. I called my loving granny, Cat, and told her how I was feeling, and she informed me that I would be leaving for the hospital in a few hours. I laid back down, but I couldn't get back to sleep. At 6:30 a.m., I called the love of my life to inform him that I might be in labor. His drunken response was "Call me back when you know for sure." I went to my brother's room and told him the same thing, and he told me to get out. Remember that I cried wolf on many previous occasions, and now everyone was treating me like I was playing. Well, I admit it was my own fault. I finally got my mother to listen to me, but she still didn't take me seriously at first. When I told her that I really needed to go to the hospital, she got everyone up, but these people were taking showers, ironing clothes, and trying to get a bite to eat—not to mention the fact that they were moving in slow motion. I was downstairs in the bathroom, trying to use it, but nothing would come out, and then the most awful pain hit me. I started beating on the walls, and I heard my mother flying down the stairs. She asked me what was wrong, and I told her that I was pushing to use the restroom, but nothing would come out. She kicked it into high gear and said, "Don't push!" Now she knew it was serious. She grabbed me and threw me in the back seat of her car and told Tee to meet us at the hospital, because she didn't have time to wait. This lady was pushing ninety to a hundred miles per hour on the highway. She ran stop signs and red lights, and I started to wonder if we were going to make it to the hospital safely.

I rolled off the elevator on the labor-and-delivery floor, breathing extremely hard, and the nurse said, "Somebody is in serious labor." I had a really nice nurse who showed me how to breathe properly. By the time I got settled in a room, everyone had arrived to be by my side for the birth of my first child. I had an entourage: my mom, Tee, my brother, Kenya, and, last but not least, the love of my life. I was supposed to be in a family birthing room, but the hospital was full that day, so we all transferred to an operating room for a vaginal delivery. The love of my life was on one side, pushing my leg back, and my mother was on the other side, pushing my other leg back. My mother started yelling, "*Push, push!*"

In a deep, aggressive voice, I said, "What do you think I'm doing? I'm pushing." I arrived at the hospital at 9:20 a.m., and my beautiful baby girl, Kadejah LaShae', made her grand entrance at 10:58 a.m. Smooth and easy! That was the worst pain that I had ever felt in my life, but as soon as she was born, all of the pain disappeared. I ended up with an episiotomy (a surgical incision of the perineum and the posterior vaginal wall to quickly enlarge the opening for the baby to pass through) but no C-section! After the birth of our daughter, the love of my life was free to go back home and sleep off his hangover. Hey, why should I complain? At least he made it for the birth. That's one thing he didn't miss over the years. Some fathers never even care to be present and accounted for during childbirth, so I should be grateful, right?

Things were a little crazy since the love of my life and I were not together, and for some reason, the word on the street was that his mother was going to try to take my baby. I don't remember where or how this rumor was started, but I had not spoken to her much since I moved back home. After this rumor got in my ear, I decided that no one was going to take my baby, and my daughter was going to have my last name. In my mind, her having my last name meant that no one could take her from me. In my defense (if I need one), I was young, naïve, and a first-time mom. The love of my life decided to tell me that he wanted a blood test to see if my daughter was his daughter. Initially I was hurt about that, but I understand the saying "Momma's baby, daddy's maybe." So I told him that he could have any test that he wanted as long as he paid for it, and we would take the results to the Clayton County Courthouse to establish child support. Guess what? He decided not to worry about the blood test and signed the birth certificate as the father. I later wished that the blood test had been completed and child support had been established through the court system, because the child support from him was minimal. I later found out that he took our daughter for DNA testing when she was six or seven years old, which was sad; it confirmed that she was his daughter, but that did not inspire him to be a better father. Young ladies, if you have a child out of wedlock, think about all the expenses that you will have taking care of your child before you decide not to get support from the father. Because it doesn't matter how good he looks, how fine his body is, or how great the sex makes you feel. Your child is worth more than any or all of that, and none of that buys diapers, formula, bottles, clothes, or shoes. You didn't have them by yourself, so don't take care of them by yourself. I can only speak these words of wisdom after I endured great lessons.

At home with a new baby, I had a routine during the day when we were at home by ourselves. But when everybody else got home, it was over. If the baby cried, my mother would come running, and she would take over. That didn't bother me, because I needed the rest. The love of my life worked at a local hospital about fifteen minutes from where I lived, so I expected him to visit his new baby regularly after he left work at 3:30 p.m. every day. Well, I was wrong. He would always make excuses about traffic down Tara Blvd. He did manage to visit about twice a week, so I shouldn't complain, right? I mean, after all, some men don't even visit their children. My simple, naive mind told me to be thankful for the two visits per week. Just settle for whatever!

I managed to breastfeed for three months, and I used that as an excuse for me to always be with my baby girl except for when I was at work. After returning to work, it became harder for me to keep up with breastfeeding, so that came to an end. Back at work, I decided to work at a different bank that offered more hourly pay. It was a local credit union, and I was excited to be working there.

After about six months, a day of tragedy came for me. I was working in the drive-through, and I made a terrible mistake. Somehow I cashed a check when I was supposed to deposit it. I gave the customer $500 cash and deposited the check. Before working for the credit union, I worked for a major bank with several branches throughout Georgia. Whenever our drawers did not balance, we would run the report at the end of the day and send to report to the corporate office, where the mistake would be found. I wasn't worried because I was under the impression that the credit union followed the same process, but they did not. When you have a corporate office and their main job all day is to find mistakes, they become good at that. But when you have two tired people who have been working in the bank all day are ready to go home, how are they going to take the necessary time to locate a mistake when they are ready to clock out? When they couldn't find the mistake that day, they found it to be in their best interest to fire me. My feelings were truly hurt because that meant that I was looked upon as being a thief. I have never been a thief, and I felt that my character was being attacked. These people did not have a clue as to who I was. My grandparents and parents did not raise a thief. I wasn't a saint, but I definitely was not a thief. If I needed money that bad, I could have come out of retirement, put on a skirt and some heels, and found a miniskirt contest at a local club and danced ten or fifteen minutes for $500. But I am here, working eight hours a day, five days a week, and you think I want to steal $500? Not me! I never had to steal anything from anyone because I had two fathers and a grandfather, and I could ask them for anything if I needed to. After terminating me, the credit union had the nerve to deny my unemployment. No, I wasn't going to accept that. I needed my money until I could find another job. I called on my father (Sidney) for advice. My father was an established union organizer for a major labor group. He instructed me to go to the library and search the laws for the state of Georgia so that I could appeal my case. My daddy is smart! Appeal is what I did. I found the information, printed the law that applied to my situation, and headed to my appeal with papers in hand. God is on your side even if you don't have enough sense to realize it. The branch manager and head teller (my supervisor) were representing the credit union, and God was representing me! According to Georgia law, they had to prove that I was intentionally negligent in my actions. I pulled out my copy of that law, read it out loud, and laid it down on the table. So where is the proof? There wasn't any proof. Truth be told, they probably found the mistake by the time we were at this appeal but were too prideful to admit their wrong accusation. Hands down, I was victorious. That manager was furious. His face turned beet red. Ha ha, devil, the joke is on you, and you have to pay up. Now give me my money! I would have appreciated an apology for falsely accusing me, but I would gladly take my unemployment. Years later I saw that head teller, and it seemed hard for her to even look me in my face. I believe she knew the truth. I always felt good about myself in that situation, because I knew that I was an honest person.

After that horrible experience, I started working through a temporary service for Georgia Pacific. My mother also worked for the same company but in a different department. I was working in an accounts receivable department, and that was my first real taste of corporate America. We had a meeting for everything—and I mean literally *everything*. We had a meeting to discuss what the next meeting was going to be about. But at every meeting, we had some good food. The only thing I wanted to know was what was on the menu. We also were able to take a lunch break for an hour and thirty minutes so that we could utilize the rooftop gym. Those were the real perks: eating and then working out. However, it was only a temporary job without benefits, and I had a baby, so we needed our benefits. Until I was able to find another job, I decided to apply for government assistance (food stamps). Yes, I wanted some food stamps. While sitting in the government office, the young lady told me that I did not qualify because I made too much money. Huh? I explained to her that the job I had was through a temporary agency, and I was only making $8.50 an hour, but I wasn't even guaranteed forty hours per week. She told me to come back if my hours dropped below forty and reapply; then maybe I would qualify. I told her not to ever worry about seeing me again; I was willing to bust $500 in the club before I came back to beg for food stamps. I was just being overly dramatic because I was still living at home with my parents, and my child and I didn't have to miss a meal. I was just hoping to have something extra on the grocery bill.

My friend Kenya helped me to get a job with a local cable company. I started with the cable company as a customer-service clerk working Monday through Friday in East Point. I was use to customer service from years of working in the bank, but these people and their cable was another story. I never knew how intense people could be when it came to watching cable TV. I have been cursed out and called all kinds of names over cable bills and disconnections. I had to develop really tough skin working in that office. I remember one incident when this guy, who was about six foot two, told my supervisor, who was a woman of about five feet tall, that he would rip her head off and stick it in her pocket if she didn't turn his cable back on. All I could say was *wow*. Cable isn't even a needed utility. It's a mere luxury.

Chapter Five
The Married Life

The four years that the love of my life was in the navy, I wanted to be married. But when he came home, we lived together and were still not married. We got pregnant while not married. We parted ways, and we got back together. For whatever reason, he was now rushing me to get married. It was like all of a sudden he was trying to meet a deadline. I never did understand what the rush was about, but I was just happy to be getting married. I wanted a wedding, but he shot that dream down because we were rushing and didn't have time to plan a wedding. I wanted a big reception to party and have fun, but that dream got shot down, too. I wanted my pastor to marry us, but my boyfriend was in a rush, and we didn't go through premarital counseling, so my pastor wouldn't marry us. Honestly, we should have waited to get the counseling. The situation may have had a different outcome if we had. But if we had not been married, then I probably wouldn't be writing this book. You will see that the majority of this book does not just focus on our marriage but also our long-term relationship and all of the mistakes made during our relationship and the unnecessary time I spent on and with this man.

One week before the selected date for us to venture to the courthouse for our nuptials, I had a vision during a dream. There was a very large snake floating in the air. The snake slithered right up to my face and stuck his tongue out at me about three or four times as if it was going to attack, and then it disappeared. I woke up terrified because it seemed so real. The first thing that came to my mind was to just pray. I knew that's what my grandmother would have done. So I was trembling and praying, not knowing what to pray for. At that time, I didn't realize what the snake meant. I didn't recognize that it was a warning of what was to come. Yes, I went to church; I prayed and paid my tithes, but I didn't have a relationship with God that allowed me to sit and listen to God after I prayed. I couldn't hear his voice! It was later in life when I received the revelation. This marriage was not ordained of God, and it was never meant to be. God tried to speak to me through my mother and Tee, but I didn't listen to them, either. Sydney, my father, didn't even know that I was getting married. It would not have mattered if he had known, because I wasn't listening to anyone at that time.

On February 16, 1995, I was married. We met at the courthouse, accompanied by my mother and his mother to see the judge. As we said "I do," only one of us really meant it! And just like that, we were married. No fairy-tale wedding, no reception, no extended family, no friends to share in this union, all at the demand of the love of my life. That night, a new life began not only for us but for our baby girl as well. When I was living with my mother, she was always around to help out with the baby. My baby did have a crib at my mother's house, but she rarely slept in the crib. My baby girl slept in my bed or my mother's bed. The point is, she was not used to being alone. On her first night away from what she knew as home, her father expected her to just willingly crawl into a bed in a dark room by herself and go to sleep. I explained to him that this was all new to her, and he would have to have some patience with her. In actuality, if he had been spending time with his daughter on a regular basis, then the place where he resided would not be a strange place to her. Instead of being sympathetic to his daughter's feelings or needs, all I could hear was "She is spoiled. Let her cry, and she'll be all right." Hell no, this is my baby, and I have been taking care of her for over a year. He hadn't brought her to his house, hadn't given her a bath, and hadn't put her to bed at night. That was not my fault. I did not want to traumatize my baby, because her being scared could have been prevented if her "daddy" had been spending time with his baby.

I understand that he wanted to consummate the marriage, but we had been consummating for the last eight years. We had known each other and been sleeping together since we were teenagers. Anyway, it's not like he spent some money for us to go away on a honeymoon. At that moment, my child's well-being and feeling of safety was more important to me, so I lay down beside her until she fell asleep, and in the process, I also fell asleep. That didn't sit very well with the love of my life, who was now my husband. He said that he was really affected by that night. We had two different views about that night. He tells people that I didn't sleep with him, and I tell people that I wanted to comfort my child first. Was I right, or was he right? I don't think it should have been a question of right or wrong. I think that two grown adults could have come to a happy medium about that night without the chaos and arguing. Take care of the child and then take care of each other. I believe that "Daddy" should have helped Mommy get the baby to sleep prior to this night so that she would be familiar with seeing "Daddy" at bedtime. I was willing to believe that we would move on from that night and start a new life, but I was constantly reminded that I feel asleep with my daughter and not him. This became somewhat of an excuse for all of his wrongful actions that were to come.

After about two weeks, I thought we had made it past the "first night" drama, but I was wrong. I was at home one day, cleaning up, watching TV, and just relaxing, when the phone rang. I answered the phone, and the person on the other end hung up. By now, caller ID was in full effect, so if you were going to hang up on me, then you should have blocked your number, because someone like me is going to call you back. When I dialed the number back, there was a woman's voice on the other end. Now, I admit that I use to be a little temperamental, so when I heard this woman's voice, I was boiling on the inside. You know how the conversation goes in instances like this.

"Who is this?" I asked.

"Who are you looking for?" she asked.

"Why did you hang up on me?"

As I continued to ask questions, I received answers that I was not prepared to hear. This woman—let's call her "Tameka"—wanted to inform me that she had been dating my husband for about a year, which was about the time that I had moved back home with my parents. We had only been married for two weeks, so their relationship had started long before we had gotten married. She wanted me to know that they were still having their sexual encounters even after my husband and I had gotten married. I know that I was stupid for most of our relationship, but if I had been dating someone for a year or more and then he married someone else while I continued to meet him to have sex, I would seem pretty desperate. I don't know who was stupider, her or myself. At least he had put a ring on it while she was still sneaking behind closed doors to satisfy her sexual urges with my husband. She had no problem admitting to me that she would meet him at his friend's apartment to have sex. He hadn't even spent money to take her to a hotel, but she felt good about herself by bragging to me about these actions. This is just my opinion, but I think that she was selling herself short; I would have demanded to be wined and dined at the best locations in Atlanta and at the best hotels if someone wanted to sleep with me while his wife was at home taking care of his baby. So maybe her information would have sounded a little better if she had dropped some high-quality names about places he had taken her instead of getting sexed up at his friend's apartment, where other friends had likely brought their side chicks, too. The killer part of her conversation was her telling me that the only reason he had married me was because I had a baby by him. Child, please, a baby? My baby is over a year old, so if his intentions were to make a honest woman out of me or if he was looking out for his child, then he should have married me when I was pregnant. Furthermore, when we had gone to the courthouse, nobody had held a shotgun to his head or mine. I let her know how stupid she was and that she could have saved both of us a lot of trouble if she had contacted me two weeks earlier, before I had gotten married, instead of waiting to call me with this foolishness. I let her know that he could have been all hers if I had known earlier.

After that horrific conversation, I called my husband to let him know about the conversation with his girlfriend. I said, "Who is Tameka?"

He was surprised. Every other woman that he had dealt with in the past would have never dropped a dime on him. He had other women trained to say the right things, but this one took him by surprise. There is always a crazy one in the bunch, and she was his crazy one. His response was not what I expected or wanted. He told me that it was my fault because I should not have called back when she hung up on me. He also told me that I should have hung up on her when she started telling me everything. I wanted his reaction to be one of protection for his wife and his marriage. I wanted him to pick up the phone and curse her out for disrespecting his wife and home. A husband who has gotten caught in his mess should be apologetic and try to protect his wife's feelings and put his side chick in her place. But that was too much to ask for from my husband. He cheated, and there was no remorse.

I was in a bad position. I had just left home two weeks earlier to get married and start a new life. Now I felt like a failure after two weeks of marriage. My family had been against me getting married, but I hadn't listened. If I went back home, all I would hear was, "I told you so, and you should have listened!" I became very introverted. I didn't want anyone to know about my situation and the misery I was feeling. The shame and extreme hurt that I was feeling was almost unbearable, and now I had to make a decision to stay or go. At that point, I decided to stay, because I was afraid of what people would say. That was the wrong reason. Don't be mistaken, I loved him with all of my heart, and the things that we had endured during our early years together didn't matter too much to me. I figured that we had both been young and stupid. But now that we were in our midtwenties, married, and caring for a baby, I expected more mature behavior. Only one of us exemplified that mature behavior. After a few weeks, my husband decided to throw out an apology and stated that he would try to be better at being a husband. I would later find out that his "better" was not the same as my expectations for "better."

We lived in a two-bedroom apartment for three months before deciding to purchase a home. We found a three-bedroom ranch-style home in Forest Park. Well, actually, he found the house. We had viewed several houses together, but I didn't have much of a choice in the decision. He drove me past a house one day and said that this was the house that he had chosen. I sat in on the signing of the paperwork and house-closing process, but I was never included. My name did not appear on the loan or property deed. It was as if I was nonexistent. My husband fed me some line about him using his VA loan, which meant that my name couldn't be on the loan. (I now know that this was not true.) I was ignorant to this situation and didn't ask any questions. I was barely into this marriage anyway, so I didn't give the house situation much thought. But for my husband, this was another control technique. His thought process was all about himself, and he drilled that into my head over and over after we moved into the house. I started to realize that the man I had married was not the fun, happy-go-lucky person I had met as a teenager. What had happened to my best friend? What had happened to the person who once bought me joy? What had happened to the happiness? I wanted that person back. I wanted to have a family and grow old together, rocking on the front porch, telling our grandchildren and great-grandchildren how we had met in high school. That dream was slowly slipping away.

The day we moved was the first time that he disrespected me and treated me rudely in front of others. His best friend was a witness to this behavior. His friend raised his eyebrows, with a surprised look on his face, as though he couldn't believe that he was witnessing this type of treatment. I don't remember what we were arguing about, but he yelled and cursed at me. I wasn't afraid of him, but I was naïve and timid, and by this time my self-esteem was very low. I knew that I was ashamed to have this man speak to me in this manner, but what could I do about it? This was the beginning of the verbal and mental abuse that I experienced. I was losing myself to this man, and I couldn't realize what was happening. I was under his control. I was forced to not have friends because he always found something negative to complain about each of my friends. He accused them of being whores, strippers, and anything else that he could think of to say about them. The bottom line is, he didn't want me around anyone who might have been able to enlighten me. I lost contact with all of my high school friends, and I never told them the reason why. However, I was only allowed to be friends with Kenya, and that was because she was his friend's wife and Kadejah's godmother.

His control never stopped. I wasn't allowed to get my eyebrows arched, wear weave in my hair, or have acrylic nails. According to his philosophy, these things we fake, and his woman couldn't be fake. I wasn't allowed to wear my hair a certain way, and my clothes had to be approved by him. My self-esteem was completely torn down, and in an attempt to regain a portion of it, I decided to pursue my love for nursing. I told my husband that my goal was to return to college to become a nurse. His response was "How are you going to do that? Who is going to pay for it? I'm not spending my money for you to go to school!" I could have applied for financial assistance, but instead of going forward with my plans for returning to college, I allowed him to shut down my dream. I wanted my husband to be happy for me and be supportive of what I wanted, but, once again, he proved his selfishness. I was being controlled and living in my own hell on earth, but I refused to go back home. No one knew my story. No one knew my pain.

I continued to attend church on a regular basis, and I felt relieved whenever I was in church. I would pray for myself, pray for my husband, and pray that things would get better. It seemed like the more I prayed, the worse he got. I felt that church was the one thing I had that he couldn't take from me, until one particular night, when our daughter was sick with a fever.

I gave her some Tylenol and told my husband that I was going to Bible study. He is her other parent, so he should have been just as qualified to watch her as I was, because that's what parents do. Parents care for their children when they don't feel well. So as I headed to church, he reminded me to keep my cell phone on in case he needed to reach me. While I was sitting in church, someone came up to the balcony to inform me that I had a phone call in the office. When I got to the phone, it was none other than my husband. There were two ladies in the office counting the offerings for the evening. As soon as I picked up the phone and placed it to my ear, all I heard was yelling.

"What kind of a fucking mother are you to leave your child at home with a fever? Didn't I tell you to leave your fucking phone on? Get your ass out of there, and come home to get your baby!" As loud as he was yelling, I knew that the ladies could hear him, because it was written all over their faces. I tried to maintain my composure, so I had half a smile on my face as I gently placed the phone down on the hook. I immediately grabbed by purse from the balcony and headed to my car, trying not to cry. When I got to my car and sat down, I was breathing hard, trying to catch my breath. The tears were flowing, and I wasn't able to control them. When I got home, we had it out. I was trying to get my church on to keep from losing my mind and possibly kill him, and he went and interrupted my time with God, my relaxation time from his foolishness. I pointed out to him that he was also her parent, and he should have been capable of taking care of his child for a few hours while I attended a church service. I was not in a club getting liquored up or in a hotel getting sexed up. I was at church!

As time went on, the phone calls from his girl kept coming. Ms. Tameka wanted me to know that she was still spending time with my husband. She would tell me, "Yeah, we just left the park, and I can prove it, because we both got a ticket for holding up traffic and playing his music too loud. Yeah, we just left his friend's house, and you know what we did there." Looking back, it is amazing to me how calm I remained during these repeated phone calls.

Finally, I said, "Why do you keep calling me? What do you want from me?" She wanted me to believe that my husband would not stop calling her and that she really didn't want to be bothered with him. Now, obviously she did not know him as well as I did, because he does not chase after women. They chase him! I told her she was lying, because if she told him to stop calling her, then he would do just that. I know that she must have been calling him, because if she didn't really want to talk to him, he wouldn't waste his time talking to her. I found out that they had met through a friend he worked with at the hospital. His friend was Tameka's aunt, and I had met her on more than one occasion. When I found out this information, I decided to contact her aunt and arrange a meeting. I was desperate to bring a stop to this foolishness. I wanted this girl to leave me alone. I met her aunt and told her everything. Even though Tameka was her niece, she let me know that she was dirty and scandalous. She said that I shouldn't let her break up my marriage. I thought to myself, what marriage? Me, my husband, and his girlfriend? Well, Tameka saw my car at her aunt's house, so she decided to call my husband to inform him that I was there visiting. Of course he showed up and told me that I had no business being there talking with her about our business, but I was trying to get some insight about this woman, so I figured that her aunt would be a good source. Her aunt was trying to talk to my husband and tell him to take care of his family and leave Tameka alone. I was glad to know that this woman was not condoning her niece's ratchet behavior. She really thought that as a young married couple we should try to work things out and be a family. That is what I really wanted: to be a family. This man was the love of my life. We had met at a young age and had become best friends. We'd had a baby together, we had made it down some bumpy roads, and through it all, we had gotten married. That's the story that we were supposed to be able to tell our children and grandchildren.

I figured if my husband didn't treat me right, then I could stay around at least for my daughter. As her father, he had to treat her right! Right? Wrong! He was the most selfish, self-centered man that I knew. His closet was full of clothes and sneakers, and I remember informing him that our daughter needed some new shoes. His response was, "For what? She has a pair of shoes, so why does she need more?"

My response was," If you can have ten pairs of shoes, then my baby can have more than one pair." His selfishness became worse as time went on. For his mother's birthday, he headed to the mall to get her a gift. When he returned, he came through the door with three pairs of Tommy Hilfiger jeans and matching shirts. Tommy Hilfiger was the style back then, and the clothes were expensive. He purchased his mother some cheap purse for fifteen dollars. Really? You spend $200 or more on yourself when you went to get a gift for your mother, and you come back with some cheesy purse for her? Oh, and I forgot to mention that he bought me a cheesy purse, too, with hopes that I wouldn't fuss about his clothes. Do you think it worked? No! I probably fussed even more.

My husband did not want to listen to anyone and was determined to do whatever he wanted. He started getting bold by staying out late or all night. One night, when he didn't come home, I called his mother. Yes, I brought his momma into the situation. At this point, she was the only person who I had informed of the whole situation. She left her house to go up and down Old National Highway looking for his car at different clubs. He had told me he was going to some club in that area, but his mother did not see his car anywhere. After that night, I told his mother every time he acted a fool. Hey, I couldn't talk to anyone else, and I was tired of holding everything inside. She was my only outlet. However, that may not have been a good idea, because her experiences with men were not that great. Her advice was just, "Hang in there, baby. I am here for you, and he better start doing right!" She just didn't want me to leave and not be a part of the family. She and I had our ups and downs, but that's what happens with family, and

I had been a part of her family for ten years. There were times when we didn't talk because she would do something to make me mad, but that's what mommas do to their children. No matter what, I never disrespected her or spoke harshly to her in any manner. I became like a daughter to her, and she wanted me to stay with her son. A lot of times, mothers don't like the women that their sons are with, but I didn't encounter that problem. We had worked through our previous problems, and now she loved me.

When we had gotten married, my husband mandated that we would pay for half of all the bills in the house, including the cell phone bill. Yes, half of everything. Were we husband and wife, or were we roommates? I knew that he was still talking to his mistress, no matter how much he denied the fact. I decided to contact the cellular company and request a copy of the bill, with all incoming and outgoing calls. They were sending the information through the mail, so I had to leave work every day during my lunch break to check the mail before he got home. When I got the bill with the listed numbers, all hell broke out. What number do you think I saw over and over again? Incoming and outgoing calls to Ms. Tameka. After seeing that number, I started—excuse my language—growing some balls. I let him know how dirty he was to have me paying a bill for a cell phone that he was using to talk to his nasty, skanky mistress. I probably used a few other choice words during this argument, but I made myself very clear. From that point on, I got my own cell phone with my own bill. When I found out he was still talking to his mistress, I took a stand and refused to let him disrespect me in my own home. When I had even a thought that he was talking to her in the house, I took control of the situation. I would snatch the phone and hang it up. He would try to go in the bathroom and talk on the phone with the door locked. So this one particular time, I found some inner strength and busted down the door. Just kidding—I didn't take it off the hinges, but I did get in and made him get off the phone. He started believing that I was crazy after that incident. I probably was crazy from dealing with him. We would argue, make up, make love, and repeat the cycle over and over. I finally decided that we needed to have a serious conversation about where we were headed in this relationship. In this country, it is very rare for a man to have a wife and a girlfriend that his wife knows about without there being major problems. And we had major problems. We sat down one day for a long discussion. It was like we were just friends talking, but we were discussing what would be the outcome of our future. I was always taught that the threefold cord was God, husband, and wife. Not husband, wife, and Tameka. My husband answered some major questions. He informed me that his father was an alcoholic and had a lot of women. He said that most of his uncles were the same way, so it was in his blood, and there was nothing he could do about it. I suggested that he go back to counseling. Yes, "back," because at my suggestion we had already had a few counseling sessions, but he didn't seem to think that counseling was going to help. I wanted to know what made him continue to talk to Tameka. Couldn't he have gotten a quiet, keep-your-mouth-shut kind of woman? He informed me that Tameka understood him better than I did. He could relate to her—those were his words. Those words cut my heart like a double-edged sword. Really? I had known him for ten years. He had known Tameka for less than three years. I knew him better than his mother did! He could sit there and feed me that garbage, which was all just an excuse for a piece of ass. After this conversation, how was I supposed to feel? If Tameka did it for him, then what was I there for?

This was my cue that he did not want to be committed in this relationship. That should have been the last straw, right? Well, the last straw came when I found a credit card receipt for a hotel. I knew he hadn't taken me to a hotel. Maybe his friend had gotten tired of him using his apartment as a hotel for free. Or maybe Ms. Tameka got some balls about herself and decided that she was a higher-class ho and demanded to be taken to a hotel. Of course, I confronted him about this, and his response was that it was from his friend's birthday, and he hadn't had any money, but he had wanted to get a hotel room to have a party. Yeah, right! By now, I didn't believe a word that was flying out of his mouth. I had to sit down and weigh the consequences. First and foremost, when you find yourself in a situation, you must ask yourself if you are truly happy. Then, you must realize that grown people cannot be controlled, and you only have power over yourself. I consulted with God, which is what I should have done before I got married. I remember watching an episode of Oprah Winfrey about marriage and divorce. What God has put together, let no man bring asunder. Oprah said that some of this mess, God didn't have anything to do with putting together. Lastly, I was at work one day, waiting on customers. An elderly lady was in the back of the line, talking about her marriage. She said that her husband had run around on her for most of their marriage. She said that she had stayed at home, cooking, cleaning, and raising their children while he had been in the streets. She went on to say, "But he paid for it on his deathbed." Wow! He lived his life just as he wanted, while she was miserable. Now she was old and gray and could only say that he had paid for it on his deathbed. Was that going to be me in fifty years? I think not. My husband didn't want to be married to me, so I was going to help him and his mistress out so that they could see each other all the time and be happy. Everyone deserves happiness. I found a lawyer and set an appointment to start the divorce process.

I wanted to divorce on grounds of adultery. I had all of this evidence: phone records, hotel receipts, and calls from his mistress. I wanted to have her subpoenaed to court and air out all of the dirty laundry. My lawyer, however, informed me that because I was still having a sexual relationship with him after I found out that he was cheating, all of that became void. Huh? Why? I couldn't believe it; I was being punished for having sex with my husband. Yeah, he was cheating, but I was still being intimate with him. Who else was I going to be intimate with? He was my husband. I was safe; most of the time we had used condoms even though he didn't want to use them. I then filed for divorce based on irreconcilable differences.

I loved my husband and didn't want a divorce. But my husband was not willing or did not know how to love me back. I thought that if we divorced, we could still be friends, and he would be able to have his other women. Yeah, Tameka may have thought she was the only other woman, but I knew better. In my little mind, I thought that maybe in a few years, he would be ready to be a husband, and we would get back together. But for now, I couldn't be married to a man who had committed adultery. We had never talked about a divorce, but it was time for us to stop living this way.

The day came that the sheriff's deputy delivered the divorce papers to my husband. He was furious. You would've thought that I had dropped a bomb on him out of nowhere. I thought to myself, *Call your girl. I'm sure she'll be happy.* I couldn't believe that he was so livid. I reminded him that his girlfriend understood him and could relate to him. Those were his words, not mine. So now he had to deal with the truth. He was losing his family because he had chosen adultery. *I* should have had the right to be livid. I had been mentally abused, tortured, and repeatedly disrespected by him and his mistress. He was lucky I hadn't snapped.

Now that the divorce was in process, I felt free to mix and mingle, so I started dating. This was not ethically the right thing to do, but nothing about this marriage had been right from the beginning. That was the excuse that I used to justify my sin, and I stuck with that excuse. I was a confused individual. I was dating and still married, but at this point I don't think I cared. The only places that I traveled were to work and church, and I wasn't meeting anyone at church. At work there was this attractive, tall, caramel-colored, slim young man. He was from North Carolina, and he talked with a Southern accent. Yes, he knew that I was still married and living with my husband, but he chose to date me anyway. I became very fond of this young man; he seemed to be down-to-earth and genuinely a good person at heart. And he was funny. I remember a conversation we once had when he asked me if I went to church. When I said yes, his response was, "I knew you were a good girl. I knew it, yeah, you're a good girl." He was so excited when he said that, and I just laughed at him. One thing he could do was make me laugh. It had been a long time since I was able to experience happiness, and it felt quite nice. We spent whatever time we could together, and he made me feel special. We dated for a few months before my first court date for the divorce.

During these months, we did some absolutely wild and crazy things. We were infatuated with each other, and we chose some interesting places to be intimate. We would go to the park and sex it up in the back of the cable truck. We would love to go riding in his Bronco, down dirt roads in the woods. And once again, we would sex it up in the back of the Bronco. We were not just having sex in the backs of trucks; we also had our share of encounters in several hotels. But it was just something about being outside and getting freaky. The adrenaline would be high, not knowing if anyone would catch us. Different men in my life played different roles sexually. This country cable man helped me to experience multiple orgasms for the first time. He also had this trick that he would do that just took me to another level, but I can't reveal that. This country cable man was showering me with unexpected gifts and dinners, and he paid half of the money for my divorce. I didn't ask him for anything. He was just so giving, and I truly appreciated him.

The morning came for our first court appearance. This was called "rule nisi." I didn't know what that meant, but it was the first of two court dates for the divorce. We would have to be given another date for the permanent docket. That didn't really make sense to me; you needed a court date to tell you when you could get a permanent court date. OK, so we did not get into any juicy stuff. Remember, the paperwork stated "irreconcilable differences." Before we went to court, my husband's lawyer had established that he wanted me to leave the home and relocate with my daughter. My lawyer assured me that the other lawyer was only doing what my husband asked of him, because lawyers know that the home goes with whomever has the child. There was nothing to prove that I was an unfit mother, so my baby would be with me and so would the house. I knew that he would never want to fight for custody, because he needed his freedom to hang out with his women.

When the judge started talking to my husband, he asked him where he thought my daughter and I should live, since he didn't want us to stay at the house. My husband told the judge that we could go stay with my mother. Then the judge asked him "Where is your mother?" He told the judge that his mother lived here in Clayton County. The judge ruled that my daughter and I would stay at the house until our final court date and that $180 would be paid to me every two weeks for child support. The judge gave my husband thirty days to relocate and told him that he should go stay with his mother. Our court date was on a Thursday. My husband was furious that he had to leave the house. When I came home Friday evening from work, he had cleared out his clothes and shoes. He was gone! On the bedroom dresser was the mortgage payment coupon and an envelope. Attached was a note from my husband stating that the mortgage was due Monday morning, and I needed to pay it by myself. I was excited, scared, and relieved. It felt like a weight had been lifted off my shoulders. I could come home calmly. No stress. Well, at least not the same type of stress. I had never lived alone, so I was scared to be in a house with a baby by myself. It was now the time to put on my big-girl panties. Look out, world—here I come. I am a survivor, and I will prove it to everyone.

I had watched my mother work hard all of my life and now it was my turn. I worked overtime whenever the opportunity presented itself. I continued to pay my tithes. Who would have thought that I could have made it through? I was working at the cable company for eight dollars an hour. I had a car note, a mortgage, utility bills, and child care. God had to be on my side. He was making a way. The road did get rough sometimes, but I managed. I continued to pay my tithes. I knew that I could have called both of my fathers for anything, but I was determined to be an adult and handle my business.

The young man I was dating soon became more of a friend than anything. After all, I was still married, so I couldn't offer much toward the relationship. He soon revealed that he was about to become a father. He had gotten a young lady pregnant before we had started dating, and the baby was almost here. The young lady did not care for me much. They were having problems that had started before I had even met him. I remember thinking to myself that I had my own drama, and I certainly did not need to take on their drama. After several months, I was told he was on drugs, specifically "crack." He never admitted this to me when I questioned him. I was never exposed to drugs, so this was all new to me. After people started telling me about the behavior of someone on drugs, I began to see a pattern. He went from clean-cut and handsome to rugged. He stopped shaving, stopped getting haircuts. He looked as though he didn't bathe. He became very paranoid. He would call me and say that people were following him, and he didn't know what they wanted. I just did not want to believe that my friend had gotten caught up. I once visited him and his baby's mother at their apartment. I don't even remember why or how I ended up there, but it was awful. The apartment was trashed, with clothes and everything thrown everywhere. Cigarette smoke hit you at the front door and wrapped around your neck until you choked. Over in a corner, in a car seat, I saw a beautiful baby boy. This young lady thought I wanted to argue with her over this man. Reality set in from the moment I walked into the apartment. If he was nasty enough to lay down with her in this nasty apartment, I knew I didn't want him. I had to tell them both about smoking and the baby inhaling all of that smoke. My heart melts for all children, but he was so adorable. I wanted to rescue him and take him home. We remained friends for a while, until he was fired from the cable company. I was told that his company truck was found outside of a "crack" house, and he was inside the house. I thought this was such a waste of a good life. He was a good old country boy. This was not supposed to happen to him. He never admitted to me that he was doing drugs, but periodically I would get a call from fellow coworkers informing me that he had been seen on a street corner somewhere looking really bad and strung out. All I could do was pray for him. I got a call from him one night stating that his mom and sister went out of town, and they had not left him with a key to the house; he had nowhere to go. He was my friend, and I felt bad for him, because at this time he had lost his job and his apartment. I picked him up and let him stay with me for the night. I let him stay in my spare bedroom, and I locked myself in my room. I could barely sleep because all types of thoughts were going through my mind. What if he stole everything out of my house? What if he got paranoid and decided to break my door down? Well, God had His hands on me. The next morning, everything was in order, so I got up and took him to the bus stop. I don't know when his family got back, but he did not call me anymore looking for a place to stay. It was over ten years before we were in contact again, and with the failure of this relationship, I again looked to my ex-husband for companionship and intimacy. Yes, he still had his woman, but I was still his wife. He wouldn't refuse when I offered, so I offered whenever I wanted. We had developed an odd type of relationship. I loved him, and I knew he loved me, but we were not supposed to be together. We were separated, living apart, and headed for divorce court. He had a girlfriend, and I was his wife. We were together whenever I wanted to be bothered, and the rest of the time, he was with Tameka. I kind of liked it that way. I got what I wanted and didn't have to put up with anything. Come over, handle some business, watch a movie, spend time with the child, and then go back where you came from. No strings attached. This seemed really simple, but there really were strings, because until we were divorced, we were still a threefold cord. Whenever we were together, we laughed about the situation. We spent the night together before we headed to divorce court. He asked me if I really want to do it, but he had not gotten rid of his girlfriend. So why ask a question like that? I figured if he was serious, he would have dissolved that extramarital situation before now. I felt that my only option was to get divorced, and if we were meant to be together, we would be together. So we headed to divorce court in love and having a good time. The divorce was final, and we met later that night to celebrate. We were funny individuals. Over the next few months, my ex-husband and I became close all over again. I thought that I was getting my best friend back. I truly felt that I was in love again after all the turmoil and heartache. I know how badly he had treated me, but I didn't want to think about the bad things. After about two months of being divorced, we were seriously talking about getting back together. We spent all day together and had a long conversation. It was going to be him and me, and he was going to let Tameka know that they were done. He chose his family and not his mistress.

Well, I stayed at his mom's house while he went to meet Tameka and give her the news. He was gone for a few hours, and I started to get concerned. He finally called and said that there was an accident and that he would tell me all about it later. Later, when he could see me in person, he told me that after telling Tameka of his plans to get his family back, she decided to claim that she was pregnant with his child. Then she decided to run her car into a tree in an attempt to commit suicide. This was the beginning of her being certified crazy.

He now decided that it would not be best for us to be together, because now he had to deal with that situation. When those words came out of his mouth, it was like he had sucked the air from my body. My legs went numb, and I began falling to the ground. He caught me, and the tears started rolling from my eyes. I remember thinking, *Why, God, is this happening to me?* The happiest moments I'd ever had were when I had my best friend, not the person who was cold-hearted and treacherous. My best friend. I wanted my best friend. God said, "If I brought you out already, why would you want to go back?" God spoke that to me, but I was not listening. I tried everything to convince my ex-husband that we could work it out, even if she was having his baby. Nothing I said worked, so we didn't get back together. I remember being in a daze, just feeling so overwhelmed. I was driving and ran a stop sign. Thank God a police officer was around and stopped me. I got a ticket for going through a stop sign. My mind was totally gone. If God had not used that police officer to bring my mind back, I could have killed myself or someone else. The officer asked me if I had seen the stop sign, and honestly, I had not seen it. I had to snap out of it for my child and myself. This experience taught me that you cannot change other people's minds, and if a man does not want you, love yourself enough to not want him. Easier said than done, right? And, by the way, there was no baby! Tameka had lied.

Chapter Six
The Divorced Life

OK. I was back in the dating scene, and, boy, did I have some interesting experiences. I started dating a very handsome young man who worked at the airport. He was a customer I had met at the cable company, and he had offered to take me to lunch a few times, and I finally accepted. Then he asked me for a real date of dinner and a movie. We had a nice time, I thought, but at the end of the night, there was not a good-night kiss to top it off. So I thought maybe he was just being a gentleman. He still continued to call me occasionally, and we went to lunch periodically, but we had no more after-work dates. One day he picked me up from work for lunch, and on the way back, we stopped at the park. He wanted to take some pictures of me standing by his car. I remember him saying that he would be traveling to his hometown that coming weekend. Weeks and then months went by, and the calls got to be fewer and fewer. Then, out of nowhere, I got a call for lunch. During lunch, he mentioned that he would be traveling home soon for a family reunion. He asked me if I could go with him to meet his family. I thought this was quite odd, considering all we did was go to lunch every now and then. Why would he want me to meet his family? Isn't that something you asked a girlfriend? He wanted me to think about it and let him know if there was any way possible for me to go. When I mentioned this to one of my coworkers, she informed me that he was gay. She said, "Kodeza, he took a picture of you by his car, took it home, and showed it to his family, as though you were his girlfriend. Now he is being pressured to produce you at the family reunion. He doesn't want his family to know that he is gay, and you are his alibi. Think about it. He's never touched you, and all you do is eat together; he really wants you to meet his family." Yeah, he was gay. Wow, a "crackhead" and a gay man! I was not doing too well with this dating thing. Once again, I turned to my ex-husband for intimacy. I used any excuse available to get intimate with him. The enemy would whisper in my ear, "It is not a sin, because he is really still your husband, since neither of you are married." The devil is a lie, and I listened to the lies.

During this time, my ex-husband's grandfather passed. For whatever reason, Ms. Tameka thought she was supposed to go to the funeral. Really? I told my ex-husband, "Hell no. I am going to the funeral, and your girlfriend will not be attending." Yes, we were divorced, but this was still my family, and I wasn't ready to let go. I had been the one going to weddings, funerals, and other family functions for all of these years. He was the one who broke up our family, not me. I would let him know when I would no longer attend family functions, and then his girlfriend could attend. On the day of the funeral, I drove up to his mother's house. Tameka and my ex-husband were standing outside, talking. I got out of my car, walked past them, and went inside. She then left, because I had made it clear to him that she was not going to the funeral. Remember, I had gotten some balls a while back. We were still having sex, so I still had a little persuasion. I am sure that she hated me that day. How do you let your ex-wife make any decisions about your girlfriend not coming to a funeral?

I held in my anger and rage for a long time. I would see this woman who helped to destroy my family more than I cared to see her. I decided that I needed to let my anger and rage out. We were at my ex-mother-in-law's house, and she was there. I remember her saying something to me, and I lost it. I wanted her to know that it was not about him. I repeatedly told her that I was upset because she disrespected me by calling my home. At that time, my ex-mother-in-law was a heavy weight. She weighed at least 350 pounds, and between her and my ex-husband, it took both of them to get me up off of Tameka. I felt better, but I had not accomplished anything. I was still divorced and still did not have my best friend back. Fighting is pointless.

Fighting does not resolve anything, and it is not ladylike. And I am a lady. But it felt good to whip her tail.

I continued to date in between being intimate with my ex-husband. I came across some real characters and had some interesting experiences. One guy I dated had me in a bad position. I went to his house after being invited by him. He said that he had recently broken up with his girlfriend. We had known each other when we were younger, and I also knew his brothers and sister. As I walked through his home, there was a picture on the wall of his daughter, another woman, and him. When I asked who the woman was, he replied that she was his sister. Remember, I have seen his sister before. I had met his sister when we were teenagers, and people do not change in appearance that much. There was not any resemblance between his sister and the woman in the picture. I wanted to see how far he would take this lie. We went upstairs to the bedroom, and while he was using the restroom, I started snooping around. I checked the closets, pulled out drawers, and discovered something very shocking. I saw women's panties and bras in one drawer. The closets were full of women's clothes and shoes. When he came out of the restroom, I said, "Are you crazy? You have me up in some other woman's house. This woman could walk through the front door and shoot me for being in her house." I also let him know that I wasn't crazy and that I remembered what his sister looked like and that it clearly was not her in the picture. I made a mad dash for the door to get to my car and never looked back. How could he have been so stupid? I don't take kindly to people putting my life in danger.

I was really getting tired of these useless and meaningless encounters, and I wanted someone to sweep me off my feet and distract me from my ex-husband. Out of an act of loneliness or desperation, I decided to contact my first love, Rodney. I was able to locate his phone number, and I gave him a call. When I dialed his number, on the other end of the phone was a woman. I asked to speak to him, and she gave him the phone. My heart was pounding, and I was so nervous, but I managed to get past my nervousness long enough to have a conversation. We talked for a few minutes, and at the end of the conversation, he asked me for my number. The young lady's voice that I had heard was not his wife's, but it was his girlfriend's, and they did live together. His situation did not stop him from wanting to see me or from wanting to take me out. We talked for a few weeks and went on a couple of dates. A lot of time had passed since we last saw each other, so we didn't really know each other anymore. But it was hard to get reacquainted knowing that he was living with his girlfriend. He wasn't just anybody; he was my first love, my true love, and I didn't want to taint the image that I had had of him so many years earlier. I didn't want to be his side chick. If I couldn't be number one, then I wasn't going to stick around. He wasn't willing to take a chance on us, so he decided to stick with his girlfriend at home. I guess too much time had passed, and the love was gone. Maybe he felt like I should've been waiting for him when he had first come home. Maybe this was my payback for making the wrong decision many years ago. Whatever the reason was, we stopped talking, and I remained lonely and desperate.

After my divorce, I seemed to attract married men, and they always had a good story. Well, they thought their stories were good. I dated this one guy who continuously told me that he and his wife were separated and getting a divorce. He stood by his lie for several months without producing divorce papers, so he had to go. I didn't bother wasting too much time with anyone. When a man showed any signs of foolishness, there was nothing else to talk about. My ex-husband was the only one who could get by with foolishness. He was the privileged one. Next, I dated a guy who was very different. He wasn't very compassionate. He came from what I thought was a good family background. His parents were still married. He was raised in a well-to-do neighborhood in a very nice home. These were good factors, but he was still missing something very important: the ability to show affection and love! I thought that I could be his savior and help him to overcome. He had a job and was in college. He was studying to be an engineer, and he strived to have the best grades in his class. Oh, I forgot to mention that he sold drugs. I couldn't figure it out, because there was no justified reason for him to sell drugs. He said that he wanted to prove to himself that he could make it in both worlds, in the hood and in corporate America. Some people just get a rush for dangerous living, and that's what he did.

Once, we were going to pick up something that he needed and almost got into an altercation on the highway. He actually started waving a gun out of his window. I had been sheltered most of my life and was not used to this type of behavior, and I was a mother. I was scared to ride with him after that, so I met him whenever we were going out. I would often talk to him about wanting to be a nurse and going back to school. Finally, one day, in a very harsh voice, he said to me, "I don't want to hear nothing else about you going to school. If you're going to do it, then do it! If not, then stop talking about it!" I believe that people come into your life for a purpose, and his purpose was to push me to go back to school. A few months later, I applied to nursing school. Because of this odd man giving me those harsh words, I was now pursuing my longtime dream of becoming a nurse. Thank you, Eric!

I was now back in college and still working for the cable company. My time consisted of going to work, church, and school. Work was peaceful because on Saturdays and Sundays I was in a large building by myself for most of the day. My shift started in the early mornings because I had to prepare service routes for the technicians. All of their work for the day needed to be printed by six in the morning. I performed several tasks, but the most important one for the technicians was submitting their payroll. Many of the 250 technicians became my friends because they wanted their money to be correct. Not that I would bribe them or anything, but they knew that I loved food. I never had to worry about what I was going to eat for breakfast or lunch. They were always just a phone call away whenever I was hungry. One particular technician became one of my best friends in life.

We became very close over the years that I was employed with the cable company. I was attracted to my new best friend, but we kept it strictly friendly because he was also married. Although he was married, he would discuss with me the other women that he dated. I would discuss my dating problems with him, and he would listen and try to offer advice in between flirting with me. Yes, we flirted, but that was it. I would say, "Boy, stop playing with me. You know you're married!" We spent a lot of time talking and eating together. He used to tell me that he loved to watch me eat. He said that I acted like I enjoyed every bite. I could also count on my best friend to always have a listening ear. I wanted to be more than just friends, but I never told him that. He was very special to me.

I met a contracted cable technician named Billy, who I believed was my soulmate. Of course he wasn't single, but he wasn't married, either. He lived with his girlfriend and their two children. I instantly fell in love with this man. When I say fell I mean *fell*. When we made love, everything else stopped. This man gave me a feeling that I had never felt before, not even with the love of my life. Let me see if I can describe the feeling. Think of the Fourth of July, when you look up into the sky and see the glistening in the night of beautiful multicolored fireworks. Nothing else matters but that exact moment in time. There were times that I would see him in the office and literally felt like I couldn't breathe. I would burn with desire whenever I heard his voice on the phone. Every moment that we spent together was special. But he still had a girlfriend, so I did continue to date other men. If he called me, I came running. If I called him, he came running. There were periods when we didn't talk, but when that phone call came, we knew what time it was.

Billy was so sexy to me because he had just enough hood and just enough business savvy about himself. He was a hustler—a hustler who got caught. Before I had met him, he had served four years in prison for some illegal activities. But after being released from prison, he had learned the cable business and was good at it. He was so good at what he did that he became the top man at the contracting company he was working for. This company was owned by two white guys who trusted Billy to run their company while they were out on the golf course. Whenever I called them about a problem, they would say, "Call Billy, and he will handle it for you." I was so in love with Billy, but I couldn't have him. He liked to play around a lot.

We were out eating one day, and I said, "I want a man."

Billy said, "Do you want me to help you find one?" And he started laughing. Tears poured out of my eyes, and the look on his face was priceless. He said, "Girl what's wrong with you?"

I said, "How could you joke around about something like that? I want you. I don't want you to help me find anyone else."

He said, "I'm sorry. I didn't know you were that serious about me. I'll never say that again." This high-profile booty call lasted for four years. Many things happened within those four years. At some point in time, I found out through a mutual friend that Billy was not with his girlfriend anymore but was living with a different woman. What the hell! How could this be possible? He wasn't with his girlfriend, but he still wasn't with me? Of course, when I talked to him, he had a good excuse. He was supposedly trying to help someone from his hometown, but it wasn't working, so he said that he was going to send her back home. My feelings were hurt, because we were still just a booty call, after all of this time. But I accepted that and continued to be a booty call. In my mind, any time with Billy was better than no time at all.

While in school, I was thankful to have my mom and ex-mother-in-law to help with my daughter. I studied day and night to keep up with my schoolwork and grades. If I took my car to get an oil change, I had my books in hand, studying. If I took my daughter skating, I had my books. Monday through Thursday was school. Friday through Sunday was work. And in between all of that, yes, I started dealing with my ex-husband again. The hope that he would become the man I wanted was still there. He used to be my husband, and he is the father of my child. I wanted to believe that there was still hope for him. Once again, we were contemplating reuniting. We were spending a lot of time together. When I had to study and wouldn't let him come over, he would really get upset. I was all about pleasing him, and there were a few times when I lost study time trying to make him happy. But no matter what I did, those old ways would resurface. He was working in Cobb County, and it was a long drive to work. There were nights when he would say that he was staying in Cobb County with a friend to save on gas. This worked for a while, because I was staying busy with school. But when I took the time to think about his lie, I started investigating. He had a nickname for me: "5-0," which is code for "police."

I showed up to his house one night when he was supposed to be in Cobb County. Guess what? Not only was he at home, but he was not alone. Yeah, here we go again, Ms. Tameka. I parked my car, walked right up to the door, and started banging like I was the police. If I were him, I would have never opened the door. He opened the door, and I started in on him. "Liar. You said that you were in Cobb County, and you're here with her?" Well, Ms. Tameka came around the corner wearing his T-shirt. I ran out of the house and to my car. At that point, he should have closed and locked the door. I returned through the front door with a Smith and Wesson .40 caliber in my hand. He was sitting on the sofa, and I was standing over him, pointing the gun at his head. I snapped. I felt that I couldn't take anymore. Words were coming out of my mouth, but I wasn't fully aware of what I was saying. Ms. Tameka thought that it was necessary to open her mouth, even though I had not said a word to her. This moment was frightening because my ex-husband had this blank look on his face. He looked as though he wanted me to pull the trigger and take him out of his misery. I believed that he was miserable. He was trapped in a world that he didn't want to be in. He had lost his family for a slut. He wanted to love but didn't know how. His dad had passed away when he was a young boy, and he was following in his footsteps in becoming an alcoholic.

When Ms. Tameka started talking, I looked over at her and said, "You're lucky that I have a child."

Somebody must have been praying for me, because I eventually came back to reality. I questioned what I was doing and then left. When I got back in my car, I was shaking all over. My mind was running a thousand thoughts per minute. A few minutes later, my ex-husband called me to inform me that Tameka had called the police to report my actions. I was really scared then, because that meant handcuffs and jail. I called Tee, hysterical, and begged him to not let anyone take me to jail. I told him everything that happened, and he assured me that no one would put me in handcuffs. He said he would take care of it, and if they were going to arrest me, then he would be there. This was a generational curse.

I was terrified. I needed Billy. I needed to feel the touch of Billy all over my body. I had to make that call, and of course, he said I could come on over. I told him what had happened, and he held me and made love to me. We had a really special and interesting relationship.

Well, I wasn't arrested, but I did have to go to court. Before the court date, my ex-husband tried to get Tameka to drop the charges. All of this legal stuff was a result of her reporting my actions. My ex-husband did not play a part in reporting me. I found out that even if she dropped the charges, the district attorney's office would pick up the case, because a gun was involved. I was losing my mind. I could not go to jail. All this foolishness…and my ex-husband and I still managed to find ourselves in each other's arms. We were both crazy. He may have been crazier than me, because if someone had a gun to my head, I would not want to be anywhere near that person. We talked the night before court, and he informed me that Tameka wanted him to lie and testify against me in court. He told her that he was not going to lie, because I was the mother of his child, and he was not going to help get me into trouble. This altercation was between him and me. It was never about her, but she was the one who had called the police. She wanted them to think that my actions were directed toward her, and that was a lie. My mother and Tee accompanied me to court. Before seeing the judge, Tameka, my ex-husband, and I had to meet in a room with a mediator. The mediator wanted to know if we would be able to handle ourselves better if we were to be in the same space in the future. We agreed and then went to see the judge. The only way the district attorney's office couldn't touch the case was if the judge totally dismissed the charges. Tee had spoken with the judge earlier, but I was still nervous. Tameka and I had to stand before the judge together. The judge was a woman, and she scolded us harshly. She let us know that our behavior over a man was ridiculous. She let us know that we were both too attractive to be put in a position to have to come to court. Then she let me know that she never wanted to see me in her courtroom again, and she never did. When court was over, I headed to the airport to catch a plane to New Jersey. My ex-husband gave me a hug and a farewell kiss. Looking back at those days, I see that we were some strange individuals.

With all of that nonsense behind me, I was off for vacation. I was supposed to spend a week in New Jersey with my cousin Junior, but the trip was shortened because I had that court date. I was excited to visit my cousin. This was my first trip to visit him, and I couldn't wait to get off of the plane. My cousin lived in a condominium with two of his best friends. I was scheduled to stay with his girlfriend, but that didn't happen. She said something about not having time to clean up. Truth be told, I didn't want to stay with her anyway. I had met her before, but it's not like we were friends. She didn't want me in her space, but she sure wanted to be with us the whole time. My cousin decided on sleeping arrangements. I would sleep in his room, and he would sleep in the basement. Evidently, his girlfriend did not know about these arrangements, because the first night that I was there, after dinner, she announced that she was tired and would be going upstairs to go to bed. My cousin had to inform her that she would not be upstairs, because that's where I was going to sleep. She turned beet red. I was thinking that maybe she should go home and clean up.

I enjoyed my vacation, and my cousin pulled out all of the stops. We ate out every day and night. We shopped several times, and I didn't have to pay for anything. We went to New York to visit some clubs, and we danced the night away. We also traveled to Washington, DC, to visit with my grandmother (Nana), Aunt Lucy, and my cousin John. The only thing that was not appealing about this trip was the driving habits of the New Jersians. I was literally scared straight every time I got in a car while I was there. I would squeeze my eyes and hold on until we arrived at our destination. And if you thought Atlanta traffic was bad, we don't have nothing on New Jersey and New York traffic. That's my opinion, but I have heard New Yorkers and New Jersians complain about traffic here in Atlanta.

My cousin was awesome! He was the perfect man. He was always kind and giving. He never smoked or drank alcohol. He was smart and could adapt in any environment.

I returned to Atlanta, and my ex-husband met me at the airport to accompany me home. In between halfway dating other men, I spent a lot of time with my ex-husband. Our time together was secretive and made up of late-night booty calls. This lasted for several months until I started dating someone I thought would be a good companion. He was an auto mechanic, and we met while he was working on my car. He seemed to be good company, and I got all of my car maintenance for free.

My graduation was approaching, and my out-of-town family would be coming for the festivities. At this time, my ex-husband and I were doing our separate things. He had his girlfriends, and I had what was supposed to be a steady man friend. My ex-husband was not a part of my graduation. This was another monumental event that he missed. My grandparents traveled from Virginia. My dad and his wife came from North Carolina, along with my cousin Tina. My New Jersey cousin, William "Junior," also made the trip along with my cousin John from D.C. I was surprised when my longtime friend from Virginia traveled to share this special day with me. Graduation day was one of the happiest days of my life. My mom had been diagnosed with cancer and was in remission, and I was finally pursuing my dream of becoming a registered nurse. We all went to dinner after graduation at one of my favorite restaurants, Sambooka's. After dinner, those of us who were younger headed to the club. Yes, we partied all night. The next morning, I didn't even know how we got home. Junior was the designated driver, and he told me that we drove around town for about an hour because my friend and I were too drunk to give directions back to my house. There weren't any smart phones with navigation back then, but he finally got us back home.

My graduation was the Saturday before Mother's Day. When we woke up on Mother's Day, my man friend asked me if I would be cooking breakfast. Really? I am a mother, and I just celebrated my graduation! You think I'm going to get in the kitchen and cook? My cousin John said, "I can tell he's not going to last too long." And last long he did not. He was quite possessive. He became the only man that I had ever been truly afraid of in my life. When he showed his true colors, I knew that he could be harmful to my health.

My man friend and I were supposed to go to a Braves game one night with complimentary tickets from my mom's job. The lady who gave me the tickets told me to make sure I used the tickets because the company checks to see if their tickets had been scanned. We planned to go to the game, but when he got off of work, he had this great idea to get a haircut. While in the barbershop, we saw the start of the game on TV. Finally, we made it to his apartment. He showered, changed clothes, and reluctantly headed to the game. I could not understand why he really did not want to go to a free game with free parking. When we got to the stadium, the game was in the eighth inning. I told him that we had to park and go to the gate to at least get the tickets scanned. He snapped! All I could hear was him shouting at the top of his lungs: "You just want to be seen. You always want to be seen! What the fuck do we look like going to a game when it's almost over? This is stupid, and you're fucking stupid!"

He drove into an empty parking lot and continued to curse me out for about ten minutes. I thought he was going to put his hands on me, and I was scared. I started praying to God, "Please let me make it back home safely." All I could think about was my daughter. What if he had killed me, and she was left without a mother? He finally calmed down and headed back to his apartment. When I got out of his car, I walked to my car, got in, and drove off as he was yelling at me for not coming inside. I drove as fast as I could. I wouldn't answer his phone calls for a few days. I then decided to speak with him so that he would know that we were over. He tried to play a guilt trip on me and told me that I was leaving him just like other important people in his life who had left him in the past. He was really presenting himself as a psycho. He stopped calling me for about a month. When he started calling again, he apologized for his behavior and wanted to remain friends. I was either naïve or just stupid, because I accepted his apology and agreed to have dinner with him. I assured him that it was not a date, just two friends going to dinner. Well, once again, he snapped right there in the restaurant. He started telling me that I thought I was too good for him, and he let me know that I wasn't all that. When I tried to speak, he yelled at me to shut up. People in the restaurant started looking at me and whispering. I was so embarrassed! I walked out of the restaurant and down the street and called a friend to pick me up and take me home. I was thinking to myself, *Buddy you have no idea who you're messing with. I have two fathers, a brother, and a grandfather who will get in their cars, load up the back seat up with a couple of shotguns, and travel from Virginia to hunt you down.* He was a true fool, and that is definitely not what I needed. I certainly was striking out in the area of love, and I always used that as an excuse to fall back into the arms of my ex-husband.

About a week before my graduation, I was told by my supervisor at the cable company that my schedule would be changing. I had worked Fridays, Saturdays, and Sundays for many years. One of the young ladies working Monday through Friday had quit, and I was told that I needed to take her position. I was sitting in a meeting with my supervisor, director, and a human resources representative. I was basically given an ultimatum: either work Monday through Friday or not work there at all! They didn't say it like that, but that is what they meant. I was laughing on the inside. I had just graduated from nursing school. Why would I want to work at the cable company Monday through Friday? When was I going to have time to be a nurse? My plan was to work three twelve-hour shifts at a hospital during the week and still maintain my weekends at the cable company. But it didn't work that way. I just decided not to show up the Monday that they were expecting me. I say they fired me, and they say I quit. Whatever happened, I no longer worked there. I didn't look for work for a whole month. I was tired, and it felt like I literally slept the whole month.

After being with the crazy man, my ex-husband and I started hanging out again. I was now a nurse, and he was a police officer. I thought that was a good combination. After we had been back together for a few months, I thought that things were going well. But we had one of those conversations that just set me back. He let me know that he would never marry me again and that he would never have any more children with me. So was I just supposed to settle for being his girlfriend for the rest of my life? He said that he was still trying to recover from the last time we got divorced, when I took his house. Oh, OK, the house that his daughter lived in with a roof over her head. I just listened as he talked and took it all in without saying a word. Time went by, but his words remained embedded in my brain. I knew that I wanted a family with a husband and more children, but he had made it clear that he would not be fulfilling those needs. I just figured that I would keep him around until something better came along.

I was then a nurse in a major trauma center in Atlanta. I loved my job, and I especially loved helping people. I now had new acquaintances— my coworkers—and I began to socialize at the local clubs and bars. One night, while heading to a club, I stopped at a red light, and guess who pulled up beside me, calling my name? It was Mr. New Orleans, looking as fine as ever. He was so surprised and excited to see me. He jumped out of his car and ran over to give me a hug. After we hugged, we exchanged numbers. We started talking occasionally, and he invited my coworkers and me to his home for barbecues and parties. His barbecues and parties were always interesting. He had many women there to see him, so he had to work the crowd. As the evening got later and later, all of these women were competing to see who would be the lucky one to stay the night with Mr. New Orleans. This sounds crazy, but it's true. He was absolutely fine, no doubt about that, and they wanted him. When they started looking at me, all I could do was laugh and turn my head. They didn't realize that the only man I had ever tried to compete for was my ex-husband. They did not have to worry about me at all, because when I finished eating the free food and indulging in the free alcoholic beverages, I wanted to go home alone. I would not be a part of this nonsense, but I did know that if I had wanted to be number one, then all of them would've been sent home, because I was the special one.

Mr. New Orleans and I did go on a few dates, and we had a few sexual encounters, but something just didn't click with us anymore. Maybe it was because of how things had ended in the past, or maybe it was because there were too many women trying to get with him. We had a conversation about trying to be together, and I asked him if he had cut his women off. He was indecisive about his answer, so I thought, *Why even have this conversation if he is still dealing with all those other women?* He was still upset and hurt about how things had ended before, and he didn't trust his feelings with me. Well, I wasn't going to hang around to be one of his groupies. I guess he thought I should prove myself to him before it could just be the two of us. So I told him that we should just be friends, because I wasn't about to go through that. And that was that. We still talked, and I still went ot his house for parties, no strings attached, no groupie here. But his groupies were still waiting it out all night at his parties to see who would be the last woman standing.

The last party that I attended at Mr. New Orleans's home went terribly wrong. I was drinking alcohol and eating, which is what I usually did at these functions. He also was drinking quite a bit of alcohol, and it was safe to say that we were both quite intoxicated. I was asked to dance by some random guy, and I took him up on his offer. Well, I guess Mr. New Orleans thought that we were too close and doing a little too much bumping and grinding. Mr. New Orleans started arguing with me right in the middle of the floor. He wanted to know why was I disrespecting him in his house. I was trying to figure out how I was disrespecting him. He was not my man, and he had all of these other women there, so why was he worried about what I was doing? Things got really heated. He was yelling and cursing, and I was yelling and cursing. Then the ultimate happened—he put his hands on me. He grabbed me and proceeded to pull me out of the house. He dragged me across the front yard and slung me around. By this time I was no longer intoxicated. The adrenaline was so high that I sobered up really quickly. I had never experienced a man doing anything like this before. I managed to get to my car while he was still yelling at me. As I drove off, my feelings were hurt, because I couldn't believe that he had done that to me. And that house and front yard had been full of people who had just watched this take place. No one tried to intervene—why? Was I not worthy of their help? Or were they just scared of him? I wanted to dial 911 and have him arrested, but I thought about my mother and his brother-in-law being long term friends. I didn't want any bad feelings between them, so I decided to just go home. On my way home, my phone rang, and it was Mr. New Orleans. I told him, "Do not to ever call me again. We are done. We are not friends. We are nothing." I never told my mother or anyone what I experienced that night with Mr. New Orleans. And we didn't speak for almost fifteen years after that night. I can say that I am a very stubborn person, and once you cross me, that's it, and I'm done. So I had no desire to ever see or hear from him again. But recently, I did decide to contact him. I wanted him to inform his sister and brother-in-law that my mom had passed. I let him know that I had seen him around town a few times, but I made sure not to get in his path. We decided to have a conversation about the dreadful night when we had last seen each other. He told me that he had heard some guys talking, and they were planning on taking advantage of me, and that was when he had lost it. I explained to him that he had lost it with the wrong one, because I hadn't done anything wrong. He should've blown up at the guys he was referring to and not me. We lost a friendship that night, because he had totally handled the situation wrong. He agreed that alcohol was a factor and that he could've dealt with the situation differently. After having a civilized conversation with each other, we both agreed that we had lost our friendship unnecessarily that night. Over the years, I have learned that friends are hard to come by, especially for me, because I am not a very trusting person. We have been able to reflect on the good memories that we had and let the bad go, so we are now friends again.

There was a gentleman that I had met earlier while working at the cable company, and we were friends for several years. We didn't see each other all of the time during those years, but we were still friends. When we first met, he was a cable technician, but that didn't last for long, because he was too pretty for that. When he found out that he had to get his hands dirty, he quit that job really quickly. To be honest, I really didn't know what type of work he did when he left the cable company. I just knew that he was always hustling something, selling cars, chasing business opportunities, and supposedly trying out for the Atlanta Hawks every year. At one point, I thought that he may go overseas to play basketball, but that never happened. We dated for a while, but we never got too serious. We became more friends than anything. We started off on a good note. You know, the usual: dating and getting to know each other. He was another tall, dark, and very built young man. I think he could've stolen my heart, but either he didn't know how or didn't want to. I remember spending an evening with him at his apartment, and he had an unexpected visitor early that morning. Any other time, I would have been upset, mad, and ready to fight, but I was actually calm. I had to get up and go to work, so I told him to make sure I got to my car, and he could handle whoever she was when I was gone. I made it to my car without an incident. I don't know what happened when I left, and I didn't really care. We remained friends after that, but I wasn't looking for more than a friendship, because obviously he was doing his own thing. He was a decent friend and seemed to be concerned about my daughter and me. Once, when my daughter was sick, he came over to help me take care of her. She was so weak from not eating. He warmed a can of soup and fed it to her. That action warmed my heart and put a smile on my face. He also took care of me when I was sick, and I truly appreciated his kind gestures. We remained friends with benefits for several years while I was in nursing school. On some occasions, the benefits included sexual relations, and on other occasions, sex was not involved.

After I graduated from nursing school, there were times he would call me when I was working the night shift and ask me to meet him in the morning when I got off. He would say that he just wanted to hold me and go to sleep. Some people don't believe that a man and a woman can lie in bed holding each other without engaging in or thinking about having sex. Well, we did. These were truly intimate moments. I think that during these times we were both tired from things in our lives and just wanted to rest while feeling the comfort of a familiar individual. Those moments afforded me some of the best sleep I've ever had and left us with good memories. Eventually the memories were all that we had left, because our friendship dissolved.

One evening, after we went out for a movie and drinks, we headed to Kadejah's grandmother's house to pick her up and head home. As I pulled into the driveway, my ex-husband and some friends of his were standing outside. My ex-husband proceeded to act as if I had done something wrong. All I could hear is, "She done brought this nigger to my momma's house."

Well, he didn't live there anymore, so it's not like I brought anyone to his house. But in my mind, I thought, *What difference does it make?*

You're my ex-husband! I got out of the car to go inside and get Kadejah. Well, when I got inside, who did I see? Yes—Ms. Tameka.

"Yo' man outside acting a fool cause I have a man in my car while you sitting in here. Can you get him please?" So she got up and went outside. By this time, he and his friends had surrounded my car and were still talking trash about me bringing a man to his momma's house. I said, "Girl, you must feel real stupid right about now. Yo' man acting a fool about his ex-wife having a man in her car. Please explain that to me?" I got my child, made my way to my car while trying not to be confrontational, and left. That night, my guy friend said that he couldn't deal with baby-daddy drama. He said that if we were ever together seriously, he couldn't handle the fact that Kadejah had to be around her father. I was kind of in shock, because I didn't think that we were planning on being together seriously, and I was kind of mad because I felt that he let my ex-husband punk him. I was thinking to myself, *Really, dude? You are six foot four, two hundred pounds, and you let him and his friends punk you, and run you off.* Well if it was that easy for him to be intimidated, then I didn't feel like I really wanted him around me anyway. We had been spending time together, becoming good friends. My daughter had even been spending time with him and his mother on a few occasions. I really thought we were friends, but that was over. We stopped calling each other, and we no longer spent time together.

One day, as I was driving, my eyes stumbled upon a house. It was an older house that needed some work, but I could see the potential. I had to have this house. It had four bedrooms, three full bathrooms, two large dens, an office. It was a split-level mini mansion. I purchased the house. My ex-husband, one of his friends, and my best friend from the cable company with one of his friends helped make the move possible. My ex-husband wasn't sold on the idea of other men helping me, but since we had been divorced, most of my friends were men. And since he wasn't trying to be my man, why should he be allowed to say who can and cannot help me move? Yeah, he was a little pissed about that, but my attitude was that he needed to get over it. He did not control me anymore.

Chapter Seven
The Billy Life

Remember when I said that I would keep my ex-husband around until something better came along? Well, something better did come along: my soulmate, "Billy." Remember Billy? I was madly in love with him from the moment I laid eyes on him.

Billy had been working out of town for about a year or so. We stayed in touch but not as often during the time that he was out of town. I was excited to hear his voice, as usual. The words that would come out of his mouth would leave me speechless. We had been making booty calls to each other for four years, but this was not a booty call.

Billy said, "Baby, I am coming back home, and I want us to be together for real." I knew that he was now single, but I didn't know where his head was at this point concerning his feelings toward me. He had caught me off guard.

He asked me if I was seeing anybody, and I said, "Yeah, but I'll get that situation taken care of before you get here!" Well, my ex-husband had to feel the wrath of Billy. I had no other choice. This man had already told me that he would never marry me again nor have more children with me, so how could he stand a chance against Billy? They were both tall, dark, handsome, and built like MAC trucks, but one of them was actually making an attempt to be my man. When I broke the news to my ex-husband, he seemed surprised, just like he had when the sheriff's deputy served him divorce papers after informing me of how well his girlfriend could relate to him. I reminded him of his words to me about not getting married or having more children. He really tried to flip the script, saying that if I had tried harder, then he could have changed his mind. His words were going in one ear and out the other. All I could think about was Billy coming home.

I told him about Billy, and he asked, "Who is this ninja who can make one phone call and get you stuck on stupid?"

I was thinking to myself, *I've been stuck on stupid with you for a long time. Don't hate because somebody else got the power.*

When Billy got home, my ex-husband knew that it was serious, because we would always mess around, no matter what else was going on. But all of that totally stopped. He was in such disbelief that he showed up at my house unannounced one night, wanting to see Billy. He wanted to see the man who took me away from him. Billy went outside, and they had a man-to-man talk, according to Billy. I don't know what was said, but my ex-husband never tried to get with me again as long as I was with Billy.

After being home for about a month or so, Billy got settled into his new apartment. We were spending a lot of time together. I had to keep reminding myself that this was not just a booty call anymore. We are really a couple. We were doing couple stuff: dinner, movies, clubs, and even strip clubs. Yes, I went with my man to the strip club. That only happened once. I had never been to a strip club with a man, so one night his cousin and I decided to accompany him to Body Tap. I knew that he went to watch strippers occasionally, but that was not a big deal to me, because when he left the club, he crawled into my bed. That night, I had a problem with feeling disrespected. He may have frequented the club and gotten table dances from his favorites whenever he was there, but this particular night, he was with two women: his cousin and me. No one knew who we were. We were just two women with a dude. Either of us could have been his wife, girlfriend, or cut buddy. This stripper walked over to our table and started dancing. So I looked at him and said, "What the hell does she want?"

Don't come to my table looking for some dollars if nobody called you to come over. So I got loud and made sure she knew that she needed to get away from the table, because her dance was free. She wasn't getting one

74

dollar. Billy kept trying to calm me down. Remember, this is the man whose arms I fell into after I had pulled a gun on my ex-husband, so he knew me quite well. I wasn't jealous. But I just don't like to be disrespected. Some people thought that I was odd for wanting to go to the club with my man. I always preferred to go to the club with a man, because I didn't like going out for the cat and mouse game. I enjoyed knowing the person I would be bumping and grinding with on the dance floor. I didn't want to worry if somebody was going to buy me a drink or if they wanted something in return. Although I preferred to go clubbing with my men, Billy was one of the few who would actually go clubbing with me. I remember one night when we went to some club and wanted a table in VIP. You had to purchase three bottles of an expensive champagne to sit at a table. So Billy said, "Let's do it!"

I loved Billy's mind. He had the qualities of a street hustler and a businessman. Billy's business was cable and Internet service. We decided to start a cable contracting company. We both knew the cable industry. I had worked in the office of a cable company for almost ten years, and he had been contracting for a while. We did our homework, got a business license, and tax ID number. Billy started subcontracting for different companies. We were doing a lot together in just a short period of time. Billy had two children, and I had my one. We tried to get our children together, but our two daughters were having a rough time with that. His son was the youngest, and I fell in love with him. I had always wanted a son. Billy used to say that I was hypnotized whenever I saw his son. He would say, "Stop smiling so hard!" I knew that one day I would have my own son. We tried to spend time with the children as well as each other, because we were planning to be together. I thought we would be together forever. I told Billy that he was my soulmate. We had the type of relationship that was just breathtaking. We didn't even know how to be mad at each other. If we argued, eventually we would look at each other and start laughing. He would say, "You make me sick with yo' lil' red ass. I can't even be mad at you." We were thick as thieves. I had a new best friend, and I was loving our new relationship. How often does that happen? You have a strictly booty-call relationship for four years, and then suddenly it turns into a committed relationship. Well, it was great while it lasted. Yes, my wonderful Billy would fall by the wayside, just like all of the others.

When I love, I love hard. If I love you, I will give you anything that I have and will go to the end of the world for you and back. That's what I did for Billy. When he started looking for his apartment, he didn't have good credit, so he couldn't get a lease. I helped him out and got the apartment for him in my name. He and his cousin were to stay in this expensive apartment and split the expenses. He assured me that his cousin had a good job, so it would not be a problem. When we got ready to start our contracting company, we needed finances to purchase equipment and get established. Billy introduced me to an elderly lady, Barbara, who sold houses. Well, apparently her credit was not good, and she wanted to purchase a home. The plan was for me to purchase the home, and she would pay the mortgage for a year and then purchase the home from me. It was a lease with the option to buy. It was a very nice house in Lilburn. It was very spacious, and there was a pool in the backyard. There was equity in the home, so when I purchased it, I was able to receive money at the time of closing. That money was used for our business. I also still owned my house from my marriage, and I needed to rent the house out. Billy introduced me to a nice young lady who was a stripper. She was so ready to move in that she even paid to have new carpet put in the house. I didn't think that it was odd for Billy to be introducing me to these people until it got scandalous. This Barbara character eventually stopped paying the mortgage. She stopped answering the phone and only communicated with me through the mail. She felt that because she had plumbing issues and had spent her money on that, then it shouldn't be a problem if she wasn't making payments on the house. I quickly realized that I had been suckered. I couldn't pay the mortgage, and I tried to get her evicted, but the process was too long and complicated. The house was eventually foreclosed, and I suppose she got put out. I was totally sick behind this situation. My credit was great until this happened. I was now headed for downfall. I guess the stripper stopped stripping, because she disappeared for a while and became a slow rent payer and then a no rent payer. After the Barbara situation, I was no longer naïve. Forget the legal system. I did not bother to try the eviction process. I told her and her father which day I would be changing the locks, so whatever she wanted out of the house she needed to get it and be gone before the locks were changed. She got what she wanted, and that was that! I became suspicious of Billy after these situations. I wondered if he had purposely set me up. Of course, he denied the allegations, but to this day I am still not sure.

When we first started our business, things were good, and then things started turning for the worse. Billy always had a story or explanation about contracts we had and then lost. The money got low, and the business was shut down. Billy's cousin moved out of the apartment, and Billy started hustling to pay the rent. His hustle consisted of having parties at the apartment and charging an entry fee. I am convinced these parties involved strippers and sex activities. I decided to show up at the apartment one night, and I saw all of these people going in and out. I stayed outside in my car, talking to Billy, and he explained that he had to make the money somehow for the rent, since his cousin no longer lived there. I'm not really sure how I felt about it at that time, but I just didn't let it bother me. When he was not able to hustle enough, I would pay the remainder, because the lease was in my name.

I told Billy that when the lease ended on his apartment, he should try to get an efficiency apartment on my side of town for a much cheaper rate. His suggestion was for us to live together! Huh? Live together? Please! I had already traveled down that road with my ex-husband. No more shacking! We were not even engaged, so why would I agree to live with him? I would be too embarrassed and ashamed to tell my parents and grandparents that I was living with some man again. My father had been ordained as a minister. I am now a preacher's kid. I can't live with a man. So Billy suggested that we get married. Although I was flattered, he did not have a ring in his hand, he did not get down on one knee, and he did not have a steady income. I couldn't say yes, not now. I told him that we should wait.

He had an opportunity to go to Louisiana and work for a cable company there to help with rebuilding after Hurricane Katrina. I told him that he should go to Louisiana to work and get established. We could have a long-distance relationship until he was able to come back. He said that he really didn't want to go, but he would so that he could get back on his feet. The time came for him to leave, so I took him to the airport, and his journey began. I was sad that he was leaving but glad that he would be making some legal money and maybe buy a ring so that we could do things the right way. Boy, was I surprised about what would come next.

Billy had been gone for a while, and I thought it was about time for a visit. I checked on flights that were affordable and called Billy to let him know that I would be coming to visit. His conversation was unusual. He didn't sound like the same Billy. You know how people sound when they start changing up on you? That day was one of the most disappointing days of my life. After my ex-husband, I did not take any nonsense from any man. Once a man crossed a line with me, there was no coming back, and I saw Billy getting ready to cross that line. I tried to stop it from getting to that point, because I truly loved that man.

When I told Billy that I had found a flight, he got quiet. I was expecting an excited response. He proceeded to inform me that he did not think I should visit. He said that he was upset because I wouldn't marry him before he left. He said that he didn't feel the same way about me, because I had forced him to go out of town to work. We went back and forth for a few minutes, and I was basically begging him not to do this. I knew what would happen when we got to that line. His view that I had wronged him by not marrying him was not changing. My view that he should go to work and get himself together before he married me was not changing. Finally, I felt humiliated. Why should I be begging him for anything? My life had been turned upside down since the day we had gotten together. There were several business deals that had gone bad. I invested and lost a substantial amount of money behind his great ideas. I was thinking about all of this as we were talking, and then the line was crossed. I was at the point of no return. I was driving while having this conversation, and my daughter and her friends were in the back of my 4Runner. I didn't want my daughter to hear me. When I reached the point of no return, I pulled that 4Runner into a parking lot, got out, and blasted him from the top to the bottom.

"How could you expect me to marry you with no job? I have done nothing but be good to you the whole time we have been together. I signed my name on a lease, paid half the rent when your cousin bailed on you, started a business with you and put up all of the front money, offered to get you a smaller apartment on my side of time, and the list goes on. But now that you're in Louisiana and you've got a little money in your pocket, you want to turn on me? OK, if that's how you want it, then let's run it. You need to get back here and get your shit out of my apartment ASAP!" Click, dial tone! This is the point of no return.

With my ex-husband, I cried for weeks, months, years. With Billy, I cried for two weeks, and then it was over. He was not worthy of my tears past two weeks. The hurt was still there, but the tears just wouldn't come. This is when I got really mean. I was a woman scorned! He would call me, and I would just ask, "When are you coming to get your shit?"

I found out that he did make a trip home. I asked him if he had cleared out the apartment, and he said that he was only able to get some clothes. By this time, my blood was boiling. I was ready for this phase of my life to be over.

He was not taking this situation seriously. So I decided to help him out. I gave him a deadline to have the apartment cleared out. Then I would be throwing everything out and turning the key over to the rental office. Whenever he called me, I just wanted to know if the apartment had been cleared. He always had a story to tell about why he wasn't able to have it taken care of. The day came that I told him to have his folks meet me at the apartment. He had to send people, because he was in Louisiana. His cousin and one of his best friends met me and also one of my guy friends. My friend was a cable technician, and I knew that he performed some cable work outside of his regular job. I told him that he could come and get all of the cable supplies that we had left over. Well, Billy's friend called him to tell him that some dude was taking the cable supplies, so then Billy called me. He had the nerve to ask me if I was giving away his shit. My response was, "Hell, no. I am giving away *my* shit, because I'm the one who paid for it, remember? And if you really wanted it, then you should have gotten it by now!" After we finished arguing over the cable supplies, Billy told me that his cousin was supposed to store his belongings at her house, but she really didn't want to, and he wanted to know if his belongings could be stored in my garage.

"Ninja, is you crazy? After the way you have treated me, after all I have done for you? Really? Do you really think that I want your stuff in my house? Do you really think your stuff would be safe in my house?" Then he asked if I could pay for him to put his stuff in storage. "Hell *naw*! You will never get one red penny out of me." When I finished cleaning out the apartment and turned the key into the rental office, I felt relieved. This was the end, and I was left standing alone again. Billy had now been added to the list for breaking my heart, after my ex-husband. No matter how much I loved him, I could never look back. This truly made me sad. My heart was crushed. I had waited four years to be more than just a booty call, and for what? For the ultimate letdown. Every couple of weeks, Billy would call me trying to talk, but I would just hang up on him. One particular time, when I answered the phone, he begged me to not hang up. Then he asked me if I could take the curse off of him.

"Curse? What curse? I am not a voodoo woman." He said that he had only been having bad luck since we had broken up. Why he thought I should care about his luck was a mystery to me. I told him that I didn't operate in curses, but how you treat people comes back to you. You reap what you sow.

I saw Billy some months after we had parted ways. He thought that he could whisper in my ear and slide into my panties, but he had no idea about the point of no return. Nothing was going to help him get into my panties ever again.

Chapter Eight
The Aftermath

After Billy and I were over, you can only imagine what happened next. Take one guess who I started dating? Yes, my ex-husband. When he found out that Billy was history, he made his move, and of course he rubbed it in my face about Billy.

"That ninja didn't want you. I knew he was going to use you then get rid of you."

I understand why he had said those things to me. He really had been hurt when I had stopped seeing him so that I could be with Billy. At this point, I really didn't even know why we continued to be together. I wasn't in love with him anymore. He had done too many things that made me look at him totally differently. In all actuality, I really resented him for many of his actions. He was very selfish in his ways. He never wanted to help pay for our child's birthday parties, but he always wanted to show up, like he was the big man on the block. The one time he did help pay for a party, it was downright embarrassing. We met at the ice-skating rink to choose a package for Kadejah's birthday party, and we had to pay a deposit. I told him that I didn't have any cash, so if he paid the deposit, I would give him the cash later. He made a big scene right there in front of the cashier and would not pay any money until I wrote him a check. Selfish! Then, when our daughter was taking dance classes on Saturdays, I needed him to take her, because I worked every weekend. He suggested that I give him gas money to take her to class. He didn't even help pay for the class. Selfish! When our daughter received her black belt in tae kwon do, he didn't bother to show up, but my best friend from the cable company was there to support us. He never contributed to the expenses from the tae kwon do classes. Selfish! When he was supposed to spend weekends with his daughter, he would drop her off at his mother's house, but if his job had a family event, he made sure to take Kadejah so that he could pretend to be daddy of the year. Selfish! I realized that everything about him was nothing that I wanted. It was time to face the truth. The man whom I once knew and loved would never return. I dealt with this reality, because I wanted my daughter to be able to spend time with her father. It seemed that during those times when we were together, he would spend more time with Kadejah by chance, because he would be at the house more often. I still knew how he felt about never marrying me again and never wanting to have any more children together. But I pushed through that as long as I could. I thought it was worth the sacrifice of having him around for his daughter.

One evening, we planned to go to the movies as a family. He complained about not having any money. Really? He went to work every day, just like I did, and he was a police officer with a paycheck. So it came out of my pocket. He claimed to not have enough gas for the rest of the week if he drove to the movies, so I filled up his gas tank, and he drove. We decided to go to the dollar movie, so I figured that, surely, since I had filled his tank up with gas, he could afford to pay for the dollar movie for the three of us. I was wrong. Then, I thought he would redeem himself by at least purchasing some snacks for the movie. Not so! After this night, I looked back over all of our years together, and it came down to this. All the lies, cheating, women, and distrust were not the things that drove me away. It came down to the selfishness. This is what made me finally walk away and never turn back. Now was truly the time, because I didn't shed any tears, and my heart was no longer heavy. I felt released from this situation. All of the back-and-forth, slipping in and out of bed with him, would be no more. I knew that I would never put myself into that situation again. It was over.

A new chapter. A new day. A new season. I was still a young woman in my early thirties. I had received a higher education. I was a career woman.

I had mothered a child, been married and divorced, and had a nice home and car. Now was my time to enjoy life.

I had never had a birthday party in my adult life so, I decided to do it up big for my thirty-fifth birthday. My cousins Tina and John were planning a big vacation that year in July, so I decided to join them. I also invited some coworkers to vacation with us. One of the young ladies I worked with would be celebrating her birthday in July also. We decided to have a party together. Our party was one week before our scheduled vacation to Jamaica. We rented out a VIP section of a club and decorated it. We had catered food and a cake. We had a blast. This was the first birthday I had enjoyed in many years.

I had to send Kadejah to stay with dad Sidney and his wife, Cynthia, while I went to Jamaica, because my ex-husband would not keep her. Because we were no longer together in any way, he decided to talk against me very badly. He suggested that I was sleeping around with all types of men. He insinuated that I didn't take care of my daughter. He always made comments that I didn't cook and that all my daughter ate was fast food. He totally tried to discredit me as a good mother. I was the one who dressed her, made sure her hair was done, went on field trips, and attended school functions, and if I couldn't be there, I made sure my mom was able to represent me in my absence. The devil will always try to make you feel bad about yourself. That is his job: to kill, steal, and destroy (John 10:10). All of these things were said in front of my child, and young children are very impressionable. I found myself trying to defend who I was to my child. Also, the devil doesn't care who he uses to try to tear you down. My ex-husband was not a concern to me, but when his evil works affected my daughter's attitude toward me, then I was bothered. I felt bad for my child, because she was confused and torn. Torn between a mother who deeply wanted the best for her and truly loved her and a father who did not know how to show true love but wanted to damage the relationship between mother and daughter. For some years, my daughter and I were actually close. Everyone told me that I spoiled her too much. I didn't mind giving her whatever was in my power to give her, because she was an excellent student. Although she may have gotten into trouble a time or two, she was very smart, so I wanted to reward her. Also, I felt guilty, because her dad was not a permanent fixture in the home. I could go on and on about my ex-husband and his lack of parenting skills, but that is a whole other book within itself. I pray that he asks God to help him.

My Jamaican vacation was something that was unforgettable from the time I boarded the plane. We were served champagne on the plane to get us ready. We were treated to Jamaican dancers in the airport while waiting for our bus to carry us to our resort. The dancers wore beautiful, authentic, bright Jamaican colors, and they danced so gracefully. After the dancing, we then took a bus ride to the resort, and we were greeted at the entrance with Jamaican cocktails. The rooms were not that fancy, but we did not plan to spend a lot of time in the rooms. We changed clothes and hit the beach. The water was clear blue, and the sand was as white as cotton. Montego Bay was absolutely beautiful. That night, after dinner, we went for a dip in the pool before calling it a night. The next day, we made plans to tour Duns River Fall. Now, I was not that thrilled about climbing slippery rocks while holding onto strangers, but it turned out to be very fun. This was probably the only time on the trip that I was sober—just being honest. It was an all-inclusive resort, so we ate and drank, then ate and drank some more. After eating and drinking, we hit the clubs. Margaritaville was the most popular club. The club was on the ocean, and there was a big waterslide in the middle of the ocean, behind the club. I was not that eager to get on the waterslide, but I was adventurous enough to meet a young Jamaican man. No, I am not Stella, but I did get my groove back! Don't let anybody tell you that sin does not feel good, because if there wasn't at least a moment of pleasure and satisfaction, there would not be so many souls waddling in sin like dirty dogs. And I was one of those dirty dogs. As a sinner, I did my job very well. Sinners sin, and that's what I did for many years, but I thank God that he never took his hands off of me.

During my trip, my newfound Jamaican love showed me the city. After taking me shopping for souvenirs and visiting tourist areas, he took one of the young ladies on our vacation and me to his home for dinner. His mother prepared a full meal for us: curry chicken, cabbage, and rice and peas. There is only one word to describe it all: delicious! Only paying patrons were supposed to be on the property, but that did not stop my Jamaican love. He was able to come to the resort and stay overnight. Before heading to the club one night, we decided to take shots of tequila at the resort. We had six shots before leaving for the club. Six shots! When I got to the club, all I could do was put my head down on a table and hope that I wasn't dying. I was so far gone, all I wanted to do was sleep right there in the middle of the club, amid the crowd and loud music. That night, I wasn't good for anything. I think that was how my Jamaican love was able to seduce me so easily. Blame it on the liquor—that's what we do, right? Then we don't have to take the blame for our actions. After that night, I tried not to drink as much, so I could actually remember my trip. Some of the ladies and I decided to have a glass-bottom boat tour; I had never seen water so blue in all my life. We were able to see all kinds of fish swimming around through the bottom of the boat. The captain of the boat was a bit of eye candy, which just added extra fun to the boat tour. This vacation was so enjoyable and much needed.

This was a year of serious partying for me with all of my new coworkers. I was socializing more with coworkers and having a great time. Jamaica was a blast, so later that year, my coworkers and I decided to have a preholiday celebration party. We had our party at a fellow coworker's home. We had food, drinks, and a DJ. It was a good, fun party. There were no fights and no arguing; it was just grown folks having fun. One of my coworkers brought a gang of people with her, but through the crowd I laid my eyes on this tall, chocolate brother, who built like a Mack truck. When our eyes locked, it was over. Although I was very interested, I've never been the one to approach a man. I was a flirter, so when he got close, I did flirt, and he flirted right back. There was instant chemistry between the two of us. He was like a breath of fresh air. The devil comes in all shapes, sizes, and personalities. This man seemed perfect. He was a young man with a good head on his shoulders. He had his own business, which enabled him to employ a few people. He was a gentleman, and he liked having fun. Well, when the party was over, I realized that I had had a bit too much to drink, and my friends were concerned about me getting home safely. My best friend from the cable company offered to follow me home to ensure that I was safe. He followed me home, and I pulled into the garage safely, but the night was not over. My friend got out of his car to check on me in the garage, and, well, let's just say he checked on me. We were both intoxicated, and we forgot about strictly being friends. Yes, it went down in the garage. Baby, at that moment I forgot about everything and let that big, sexy, brown-eyed cable man have his way with me. This man put it on me, and I was weak at the knees. All I was thinking was, "Boy, why do you have to be married?" That encounter led us to a serious conversation, and we decided that it was the liquor and not us acting rationally. We decided to remain friends and never allow ourselves to give in to the lust again. I knew that would be hard, because I was madly attracted to this big, sexy cable man.

Back to Mr. Tall and Chocolate from the party. We started dating, and although it was just for a few months, it felt like we had known each other for years. We stayed on the phone for hours at a time. I worked at night, and he would stay up to talk to me when I took breaks. I would tell him to go to bed and get some sleep, and he would say, "I can sleep when I'm dead, but since I'm alive, I want to talk to you."

I let this man into my world. He came to Thanksgiving dinner with my family, and he did something very special. He brought me flowers and brought Khadeja a gift. I thought that I had struck gold. His parents pastored a church, so I knew that he had been raised right. I wasn't in love with him, but I thought that we would grow together and pursue a relationship. Well, some people say that all good things must come to an end. I say that God will let every hidden thing be revealed (Luke 8:17 and Mark 4:22).

One evening, as we were going out, he decided to reveal to me his marital status. We had been spending so much time together day and night. I had been spending the night with him at his apartment. Who would have thought that he was married? Wow! OK, so he revealed that he was married, separated, and headed for divorce. Now, here comes the good part. Because he had been in a long-term relationship and now was essentially free, he was not ready to commit to another relationship. He let me know that I was a good person, and I deserved better than what he had to offer. He suggested that we just remain friends. All of this was "code" for "I want to keep sleeping with you, but I don't want to commit, because I want to sleep with everybody else." These are the games of the world. I decided to play the game, because he was fine! So I allowed myself to be a booty call once again. While being a booty call, I was frequenting the club scene once again. My best friend was a bouncer in a club, and I always got in the club where he was working without having to pay. He would buy me drinks and take care of me. The club scene never seemed to change. Every weekend was the same thing and the same people showing up and trying to run game.

One night, as I was sitting at the bar in the club, I just looked around at every one and started wondering why I was there. Was I trying to meet someone? Or did I just come to spend time with my best friend, who I couldn't have anyway? I decided that I was no longer interested in being in that environment, so I got up, found my best friend, kissed him on the cheek, and said good night. And just like that, I felt like I didn't need to be in the club scene anymore. I remember a sermon that I heard Mason Bethea preach during the time he was a pastor. He said that there is a season for everything, even sin, and at some point, the season will end. I felt this was the end of my clubbing season.

In the midst of being a booty call, I got pregnant. What? I was pregnant by a man who did not want to commit. How could I call him and tell him this piece of news? I built up the courage and finally made the call. He handled it pretty well at that moment, but things got more intense in the weeks to come.

On my weekly trip to the hair salon, while sitting under the hair dryer, I was minding my own business when my pastor walked in. I had not been to my home church in quite some time. My schedule was hectic, and I was working at night. When I worked Saturday nights, I would work from seven at night until seven in the morning. After work, I would go to an eight o' clock service at Mason Bethea's church and be home by ten in the morning so that I could get some sleep and be back at work at seven at night. I had first joined my home church back in 1993, while dating the love of my life. I had been an active member, serving as a greeter and on the nurse's gill. But now I was missing in action. My pastor tapped me on the shoulder and said, "Sister Kodeza, how are you?" The conversation ended with him giving me his number. He asked me to give him a call. I prepared myself to answer questions about not being at church before I made that call, but the call wasn't about coming to church at all. He wanted to know if I was aware of the situation with him and his wife. I told him that I had heard some things about them being separated. He told me that he wanted to be able to talk with someone about the situation who was not at the church and who did not have an opinion about the situation. Because this book is my life story, I chose not to discuss what he revealed to me about his marriage and separation. My life story only displays things that I have endured directly. He talked, and I listened, and I revealed to him the person I was having a sexual relationship with. He actually claimed to know the parents of the gentleman, because they pastored a church. He said that he thought my partner was somewhat of a ladies' man. I didn't think much of that comment at the time. We began talking frequently, and I suppose it was therapeutic for him. I also didn't mind helping my pastor.

Things started taking a turn rather quickly with my pregnancy. On my first doctor's visit, my physician did an in-office pre-ultrasound. As he was looking at the monitor, he said, "Wow. You're having twins."

What? Twins! What! Now I had to call this man and tell him that we were having twins. This was too much for me to handle. My mom was fighting her own battle with breast cancer and was recovering from a double mastectomy and reconstructive surgery. I called on my faithful Auntie Joyce to comfort me during this time. My aunt accompanied me to the next doctor's appointment. When I left that appointment, my whole world was turned upside down. The words that came out of my doctor's mouth left me speechless. When we got into the elevator, I finally told my aunt what I had been told.

My doctor said, "Either you are having multiple babies, or something is terribly wrong." What? I wanted to know the likelihood of something being terribly wrong. My doctor felt confident that I was having four babies, but for precaution I needed to have a specialized ultrasound. Well, Auntie Joyce was ecstatic. She was making plans to take at least one or two of the babies for herself. Although I wasn't prepared for four babies, I didn't know how I could part with any of the babies. I would probably need several people to live with me and help me with the babies. The emotions running through my body were overwhelming. I went from two babies to four babies in one visit. The babies' daddy was going crazy. He kept saying, "Kodeza, how am I going to take care of four babies? What about college for four people at one time?" He was thinking way in the future, and I just wanted to cope with right now. This was very shocking to both of us, considering we weren't even together, only sexual partners. He may have believed that I was not being truthful, because he decided to accompany me to the next doctor's appointment, which was the specialized ultrasound.

The day of the ultrasound was very emotional. As I climbed onto the table, I was the mother of four babies. As I got down off the table, I was no longer the mother of those four babies. Let me explain. The doctor performing the ultrasound informed us that I had a molar pregnancy. A molar pregnancy occurs when a nonviable fertilized egg implants into the uterus. This is a gestational trophoblastic disease that grows into a mass in the uterus. There are two types of molar pregnancies, complete or partial. I had a complete, which means sperm combines with an egg that has lost its DNA. A complete molar has a higher risk of developing into choriocarcinoma, a malignant tumor of trophoblast cells. Cancer.

We were both sitting in this office, listening to the doctor explain everything. This was her short version of the situation: "Your pregnancy is not viable. This is a dangerous situation, because you could have cancer cells spreading in your body. The pregnancy has to be terminated as soon as possible. If cancer develops, it could quickly spread to your lungs and brain. You will need to see your ob-gyn today or tomorrow to schedule your surgery. You will need to have a chest x-ray to check for any abnormalities that would suggest further screening for cancer. Lastly, you will need to return to your ob-gyn's office every week to have your blood tested to make sure the human chronic gonadotropin, or HCG, levels decrease to zero." Whew. That was a lot to swallow. All I heard was no babies and cancer. I broke down crying. The doctor and my sexual partner tried to comfort me, but I don't think their efforts helped very much. My head was spinning, and I was literally sick to my stomach. God, why me? Cancer! My mom had just gotten out of the hospital after having a double mastectomy. Now I may have lung or brain cancer.

My mother and I did not have the greatest mother-daughter relationship for many years. We disagreed and argued over any and everything. We were better with each other when we did not invade each other's space. Maybe it was just too much estrogen, or maybe the devil just wanted to keep us at odds. When I left the doctor's office, I asked God to forgive me, and I immediately called my mother and told her the whole situation. I apologized to her for any and every thing that I had said or done wrong toward her, and she forgave me. My mother was still recovering from her surgery, so Auntie Joyce and my uncle, Lil' Daddy, accompanied me on the day of my surgery. My babies' daddy, who was not my babies' daddy, was supposed to meet me at the hospital on the day of the surgery, but I never heard a word from him. Not one word! He was missing in action. I made several attempts to contact him, and I was unsuccessful. I remember thinking on the morning of my surgery, "How could this man act like this at such a crucial time? I have been treated really awfully by the love of my life, but I don't believe that he would even do something this low down." Well, I had my pastor's support. He talked to me before and after the surgery, and I informed him of my sexual partner's actions. My sexual partner and I had already established that we were not going to be in a relationship, but I did expect a little friendly concern.

I thank God for his angels. My aunt was by my side, praying. Before going into surgery, my doctor came in the room and asked if I would allow him to say a prayer. There are angels watching over me! Yes, Lord! I could not appreciate my angels at that time, but looking back now, I know that I was truly blessed. How many doctors ask their patients if they can pray with them before going into surgery?

The surgery was over, and it had gone very well. Still, I had not heard a word from my sexual partner. After numerous attempts to reach him, I decided that it was not worth my time to continue to use my energy to dial his number. Karma! That's all I have to say.

Chapter Nine
The Transformation Begins

My surgery was three days before Christmas, and that meant that I was off from work for a few weeks for the holidays. I was falling into a depression, but my pastor continued to talk to me through this difficult time in my life. My pastor thought that it would be a good idea for me to get out of the house and get some fresh air, so he invited me over to his home to help him wrap Christmas gifts. I was impressed with his big, beautiful six-bedroom home in a gated community. After touring the house, we settled in the basement to wrap gifts. He had this very nice pool table, and he asked me if I could shoot pool. It had been years since I had engaged in a game of pool, but I figured the skills would easily return, just like riding a bike. As we were halfway through the game, he had a question for me: "How would you feel if I asked you for a kiss?"

I thought, *What? You're my pastor! Why would you want to kiss me?* Then I opened my mouth and said, "I guess that would be OK." Why did I say that? Maybe I felt like I needed comforting after the miserable couple of weeks that I had just endured and being dumped by the wayside by my sexual partner. I felt that I needed that attention. After all, he was a man of God. Who would have thought that I was really worthy of his attention? So we kissed, and it was gentle, sultry, exciting, sexy, and seductive. Was this the beginning of something special? Everything instantly changed. He was no longer just my pastor. Now he was my friend. Our relationship extended past church. We would never be the same again. A week later, on New Year's Eve, I attended the watch-night service, and my ex-husband was also there. The pastor announced that he and his wife had been officially separated for two years and were headed for divorce. At the end of service, my ex-husband walked over to me and said, "What are you doing here? Putting in a bid for the pastor?" I just smiled. Little did he know, my bid was already in, and I hadn't even made the first move.

Before our relationship went any further, I prayed a prayer to my heavenly Father.

"Lord, I am not what I should be, but I am not what I used to be. I am tired of all the games in this world with men and relationships. I have been married, and the marriage failed. I have dated several men in my life, and I have not had a successful relationship with any of those men. Lord, I want a godly man so that I can experience the right type of relationship with a good man. I want a husband who loves you first and will know how to love me, his wife," I prayed. We have to remember that when we start speaking, the devil is also listening, so we must pray for discernment. After I prayed this prayer, I heard God say, "I have a man of God for you."

My pastor wanted to spend more and more time with me, and I agreed. He was filling a void. We had gone to lunch and dinner a few times, but our first real date was at the Fox Theatre to see The Nutcracker. This was my first Nutcracker experience. This man was showing me things that were new and different from my normal. When I noticed that he wanted to spend more time with me, I questioned him, asking, "Are you sure this is what you want to do? What will people think? I was just in the clubs a few months ago!"

His response was a question for me: "Do you plan on going back to the clubs?"

I said, "No."

He said, "OK. Then it doesn't matter." Was he trying to be my savior? Did he really care for me? Or did he have an ulterior motive? Was there a hidden agenda? He was eighteen years my senior and was more mature than any man I had dated in the past. He opened doors, pulled out chairs, and brought me flowers! His nickname for me was "Baby Girl," and

I called him "Boss Man." It seemed a little odd at first, but we quickly became good friends.

After we had been dating for a few months, he let me know that he wanted me to come back to church. I was still attending morning service at Pastor Mase's church, because I was still working the night shift. But I decided to make a sacrifice and lose sleep, because he wanted to see me at church, and he wanted me to start serving on the nurses' gill. Even though I had been a longtime member, I had never graduated from the new members' class, so I had to attend the class before I could become active in church again. I didn't think this was fair, but he convinced me that it was necessary. He began molding me to be his spouse. He questioned my choice of music, because I was still listening to the popular V103, so he challenged me to only listen to gospel and Christian music for thirty days. I found that there were a lot of gospel artists with good, upbeat music. I love music, so I thought that this challenge would be extremely difficult. By the end of the thirty days, I was more appreciative of gospel music. I still listened to V103 from time to time, but I became more aware of the lyrics I was hearing.

We dated secretly for a year. People would speculate about us, but they were never certain. Somehow my ex-husband found out that I was dating my pastor, and he did not handle that very well. He was the one who had introduced me to the pastor and this church. My ex-husband decided to show up one Sunday during service and acted like a fool. He wanted to discuss why Kadejah was at church and why she didn't want to go with him. I was confused; isn't it a good thing if your children want to go to church? He decided to bash me in front of several church members and announced that I was dating and sleeping with the pastor. He was so angry and threatening. He stated that he would "bring the heat." He was a police officer with a gun, so I took this to mean that he would show his firearm. I was so embarrassed and just simply shocked. My legs turned to spaghetti, and I felt myself falling to the floor, but someone caught me and placed me in a chair. One of the associate ministers was also a police officer and informed my ex-husband that he was going to leave the church, but it would be his choice if it was going to be the easy way or the hard way. My ex-husband did leave without being forced, but he grabbed my daughter and took her with him. I was truly worried about her, because he was in a mad rage. My heart was beating so fast, and I was shaking uncontrollably. When I finally calmed down, I decided to leave church and go home, hoping he would bring my daughter to me. Well, he finally brought my daughter home that night. My ex-husband blasted me about my relationship with the pastor. He said that I had betrayed him by dating his pastor. Really, brother? When was the last time you were even at church? When was the last time you paid tithes? When was the last time you even had a conversation with the pastor? Now, all of a sudden, he is your pastor, and I betrayed you. Whatever! You are just jealous and mad because I don't want you anymore. This was not about your pastor; it's about you and the fact that you no longer have control over me.

We continued to have arguments about my relationship with the pastor until one day he showed up at my house, banging on my door while yelling at me. I was not dumb enough to open the door. Instead, I called Tee and told him the situation. Tee called my ex-husband on his cell phone and had a conversation with him. All I know is after that conversation, my ex-husband backed out of my driveway and has never spoken to me again. I always thought that it was a sad situation that we could not be cordial enough to coparent our daughter. He displayed so much anger and hostility toward me. I wish that we could have gotten along long enough to raise our daughter without so much confusion.

The first time that my pastor boyfriend and I were seen in public by church members was at the Annual Christmas Gala. We prepared for that night. He chose my dress, because it had to be perfect, right down to the shoes. I spent weeks searching for the most fabulous shoes and accessories. We were officially a couple, and this was our coming-out party. Everyone anxiously anticipated our arrival. "Are they coming together? What will they be wearing?" were the buzzing questions of the evening. We finally arrived, and everyone was so happy to see us together, or at least they made us think so. Everyone was smiling and telling us how nice we looked. I felt special, just like a princess in a fairy tale. We were a secret anymore! But he was still married. This was a confusing situation, because people in the church wanted to see him happy, but it still wasn't right, because he was still married.

That night was the night that I met someone who became a good friend. She was here visiting all the way from South Africa. She was recently engaged to a fellow church member. We instantly became friends and remained friends for quite some time, although we have now lost touch. The four of us did some double dating, and we enjoyed spending time together as couples.

We were now spending time together at family functions, before and after church and everywhere in between. When we began discussing a long-term relationship, the subject of having more children was a big topic. He told me that having more children was not something that he had thought about. Most of his children were grown, except for his baby daughter, who was around ten years old. I expressed that I would like to have a baby whenever I remarried. He told me that if it was my desire to have more children, he would have to give it some thought and consideration. He explained to me that getting a divorce and having to date and remarry was not how he had planned his life, but now, he now had to redirect his thinking. At this point in time, it sounded like we were pretty serious. At least, that is what I was led to believe. This was crazy; my pastor was my boyfriend. I would have never imagined this happening, but it was kind of cool. I felt myself becoming a more mature Christian woman. I became more attentive to the preached word, not just from him, but from anyone who was preaching. I began taking more notes during church and studying more. I wanted to know more details about the Bible, such as time frames, geographical locations, who wrote what, and so on. My boyfriend told me that I did not need to get that detailed, because I was not a preacher. Well, I thought that was a bit odd. I felt like he had just cut me down, so I stopped trying to learn such detailed information. I was a baby in Christ, yearning for information, knowledge, and a deeper understanding of the things in the Bible that were supposed to be my blueprint for living. I wondered why he felt that my knowledge should be limited, but I did not pursue the matter. I just trusted that he knew best, because he was the man of God, my pastor, and my man. Maybe he felt that if I was well informed and built a closer relationship with God, then he would not be able to execute his plan. This is merely a speculation, because I don't know what was going on in his head. I only knew the things that were spoken to me.

After months of waiting, his divorce was final, and now we could really discuss getting married. You know, doing the right thing. As I talked about marriage, he talked about birth control. Yeah, that's right. He wanted to know if I was using or taking any birth control pills. Well, we had been together for a year. We were not having sex, and I wasn't having sex with anyone else, so I didn't feel the need to be on any method of birth control. He suggested that I go to the doctor to get some birth control pills. That was his way of letting me know that he wanted to have sex with me. I told him that the pills made me sick, so my form of birth control for many years had been condoms. Remember, the title of this book is *A Transparent Transformation*, so if you are not able to read the rest of this book without being judgmental, then please put it down. I speak the truth, because that is what God placed in my heart.

During a time when I was broken and had gone through one disappointment too many with men and relationships, this man came along. A godly man. I figured that the men of the world did not mean me any good, so this godly man must be a lot better than these worldly men. I fell prey, and I decided to give my heart and body to this godly man. This man who led me to believe that he loved me and wanted to marry me. No, he did not put a ring on it, but I still laid down with him in intimacy. I never quite felt comfortable with the situation, but I went along with it. We were always intimate in other areas of his house but never in his bedroom. Maybe that was his way of keeping his room holy and sanctified. I managed to convince myself that on Sunday mornings and Wednesday nights, this was no longer the man I was sleeping with or my boyfriend, but my pastor. He sure could preach, and I have to admit that I learned a lot from his teachings over the years, even before he was my boyfriend.

During my earlier years of going to church, I had not been very involved with individuals. I was happy just going to church, sitting in the balcony, listening to a good sermon, and going back home. I was the first one to hit the door when service was over. I was never involved in church gossip or messes, because I got out of there. But while dating the pastor, I found out about the other side of church business and church folk. Yes, church folk! People didn't realize that I saw them whispering whenever I walked into the room. They watched how I walked, the clothes I wore, the words that came out of my mouth, and how I praised God. But they didn't know that Kodeza knew how to stand by herself. I wasn't associated with many women. I was able to take myself to a restaurant and eat a five-course meal alone. I went to the movies by myself and enjoyed my own company. So, certainly I could go to church with my head held high while they whispered among themselves about me. My point is that I was not intimidated. I had acquired tough skin. I found that some church folk only knew you at church. But in the streets, they try to go in the other direction, or all you get is a dry "Hey." I often wondered which Jesus were these types of people were serving. Several individuals formed an opinion about me without even knowing who I was. There were some who believed that I was not right for their pastor. But others felt that he was happy at this time with me, so they were happy for him. Some would say, "She is pretty, but she is not first-lady material." Ha! What is first-lady material? Well, I was told that I should wear certain types of suits and big hats. I was told that I have to sing in the choir. Oh—this was the best one—I had to be ready to preach.

These words were not just coming from my fellow church folks, but from other church folks that wanted to school me when they found out I was dating a pastor. Then there was the ultimate question: "Why do you want to be a pastor's wife?" First of all, I had never set out to be a pastor's wife. I had been sitting under a dryer, with a head of wet hair, when he had tapped me on the shoulder and said, "Sister Kodeza." I was doing my own thing, which had nothing to do with him or any pastor. Yeah, that whole experience made me search to understand what God wanted me to do and who he wanted me to be with. I was embracing this godly man I believed was for me, which meant that I had to embrace the fact that he was a pastor.

As time passed over the next year, the proposal never came. Our routine was pretty consistent until the last two months of our relationship. Our friends were getting married in September, and we were both part of the wedding party. I was one of the bridesmaids, and he was one of the ministers conducting the ceremony. I now believe that he tolerated our relationship until the wedding was over, so there wouldn't be high levels of tension between us on our friends' special day. Leading up to the wedding, his pattern began to change. We used to talk all times of the night, but now, after 8:30 p.m., he stopped answering the phone. He would say that he was tired and went to bed early. We stopped going out as much. If I had been dating a worldly man, I would have caught on very quickly. But this was my godly man and my pastor; I had him on a pedestal. He would never lie to me or cheat, so I didn't pay it much attention. Then, on the day of our friend's wedding, I saw a different man. This man, who had never raised his voice at me, who had brought me flowers, who opened doors and pulled out chairs, who treated me like a queen, made a total turnaround. When my friend and I arrived at the church, no one was there, and the doors were locked. We drove to a nearby store, and I called him to tell him the situation. This man yelled at me, saying, "What do you want me to do? Why are you calling me with this? I'm not there, so just wait until somebody shows up!" I froze. As I held the phone tight to my ear—I didn't want my friend to hear this foolishness on her special day—I just smiled, because she was looking at me. For a minute, I had a flashback that I was dealing with a worldly man. Remember, at this time I had only been on this Christian walk for two years, and in my mind, I forgot I was a Christian. If my friend was not there listening to me and watching my responses, he would have seen the College Park queen resurrected. I wanted to tell him, "Who the hell do you think you are talking to like that?" But I continued to smile, said OK, and hung up the phone. My blood was boiling. My friend wanted to know what he said, and I told her that someone was on the way to let us in the church. We made it through the wedding, but at the reception, we never managed to sit at the same table. Just a year earlier, we were the talk of the town as he escorted me to the Christmas Gala. There was a change, but I was convinced that God would let every hidden thing be revealed.

As things were coming to an end with the preacher man, I decided to reach out to my best friend from the cable company. He and I decided to once again cross the friendship line, and I enjoyed every moment of it. The preacher was acting crazy, and the cable man was handling business, not cable business. We were officially over the friendship line, and that caused a problem. There were new expectations, new wants, and new desires that went way past friendship.

At this time, my best friend was still married, but he was separated and headed for divorce. I didn't have anything to do with that, because I had been with the preacher for the last two years. I wanted to be with my best friend, but my expectations, wants, and desires were way ahead of his. I was visiting him frequently, and the feelings that I had for him continued to grow deeper. Well, really, my feelings were already deep, but I had never allowed him to know my true feelings, and that was a mistake. It felt like his divorce was in slow motion. I wanted to tell him how I felt about him all these years that we were friends, but I didn't. Instead, I was impatient, mad, frustrated, and disappointed. I remember listening to him talk about spending time with his wife and kids, and I think that he forgot we were not just friends anymore. I wanted so much more from him. However, I kept my feelings and thoughts to myself, and I disappeared. I wouldn't call him, and I stopped answering his calls. Eventually, he stopped calling, and I never gave him an explanation as to why I had disappeared. Just like that, I lost my friend again, but most importantly I lost someone whom I cared for deeply, and he never even knew how I felt. I later regretted not sharing my feelings and thoughts with him. We drifted apart, never to have contact again, but I always thought of him.

The time that I spent with the preacher was now minimal, and we were no longer intimate. Sundays after church, our routine was no longer the same. We did not go to dinner. We went our separate ways. Then the phone call came Monday morning. Yes, it was a phone call. He was not even man enough to have a face-to-face conversation.

"I know you want a baby, and I've decided that I don't want one. I have to do ministry and can't be worried about a baby. I have to travel to speaking engagements, and little kids slow you down. I know how important that is to you, and I know that God will give you what you want." As he spoke, the tears rolled down my face. Was my heart broken because I was in love? No, I was broken. My self-esteem took a dive to the floor. If I can't sustain a relationship with this godly man who I believed was for me, then what good am I? I got mad because he had just changed my life and my routine for the past two years. I said, "OK, if that's how you feel, then it's no problem. But know this: I have become a godly Christian woman, and what you have done will not set me back. I will not be back to your church, but I will continue to seek the word, and I will be in somebody's church. I am not going to run back to the clubs or subject myself to meaningless relationships." And that was that, in one phone call. I realized that I had just wasted two years of my life.

I was trying to drown my hurt and disappointment in liquor and then sex. I was also promiscuous and found myself with two sex partners. And, once again, I became pregnant. I wasn't sure who the father was. I only revealed this information to one of the potential fathers, because I wanted and needed him to escort me to the clinic, and he did. I told him that he wasn't the only possible father, and he told me that he didn't pass judgment on me for that. He seemed pretty understanding about the situation, and he was very supportive.

I thank God for true friends who allow themselves to be used by God. My friend whose first wedding I was in had many conversations about this situation with me. She said, "Kodeza, you have to find the good in it. You don't talk the same way you used to. You don't walk the same way that you used to. You don't think the same way that you used to. This experience was necessary to prepare you for your true man of God." Well, I didn't want to hear that, because I didn't want any more godly men. If a godly man can do me wrong like a worldly man, then what was the point? That was how I felt. I felt better being in sin and getting disappointed than being with the pastor still getting disappointed. I slowly found myself doing what I vowed not to do. I was going to church, but I found myself drinking and back in the club.

I remember being out with him, and after I'd had too many drinks, he had to help me to the car. I said, in a drunken slumber, "What if I'm really supposed to be somewhere, preaching?" Then I started laughing.

He said, "Then I will go with you." I don't know if he was serious or not, and he probably thought that I was crazy. One day I broke down and said, "God, what happened? You said you had a godly man for me."

Then God said, "You didn't wait for the rest of the conversation. I didn't say that he was the one."

"OK, God, I am going to stop doing what I am doing. I surrender to you. Now give me my godly man."

Two weeks later, I received a phone call from a friend, who said she wanted me to meet her boyfriend's uncle. She said, "He's a preacher."

I said, "Hell *no*. I don't want no more preachers."

She said, "Don't miss out on your blessing, and just talk to him. He's a nice and kind man."

So I said to her, "OK. You can give him my number."

We talked on the phone for two weeks before we ever met in person. He told me that I was going to be his wife. I told him he didn't even know me. He said, "I know your spirit."

Dedication

I would like to thank all my family, who were supportive and encouraging during my time working on this project. This book is dedicated to special individuals who are no longer here with me working on this project. This book is dedicated to special individuals who are no longer here with me:

Ethel Mae Young, my mother;
William Young Jr., my cousin;
Roy Gunter, my grandfather;
Pamela Young, my dear friend;
and to Herbert Nicholson. You were my grandfather, and I loved you without knowing you.

These are my guardian angels, always and forever.

About the Author

In 1970, a child named Kodeza Young was born. She is a Christian and has maintained the role of wife, mother, and grandmother. From an early age, Kodeza exemplified a passion for educating and caring for others. Through this passion, she exercised her skills and talents in several areas of nursing. During her journey through life, she has endured many hiccups, hang-ups, and screwups. In an effort to enlighten women to recognize their self-worth, she was led to share her journey. Sit back, relax, and enjoy the life experiences of Kodeza Young.

Made in the USA
Middletown, DE
15 February 2020